GROWTH INDUSTRIES IN THE 1980s: conference proceedings, sponsored by the Federal Reserve Bank of Atlanta. Quorum Books, a div. of Greenwood, 1983. 196p bibl index 83-13822. 35.00 ISBN 0-89930-069-3. CIP
Conferees were concerned with identifying characteristics that differentiate growth industries from those experiencing stagnant or declining growth. The participants included corporate executives, the financial press, management consultants, e.g., Roger Waterman Jr. (coauthor of *In Search of Excellence: Lessons From America's Best Companies*, CH, May '83), and social critic Alvin Toffler (*Future Shock*, CH, Jan '71). The emerging growth industries include manufactured housing, medical services, and a variety of industries built around the computer such as computerized shopping, automated office equipment, and information systems. The individual contributions are brief and uneven in content. Although the topic "growth industries" is the common thread, the individual contributions lack focus and are not unified by a more specific theme. Several are very narrow, discussing only the individual participant's firm. The book's strongest section, "Key Growth Characteristics," identifies factors that help explain why some firms are successful while others fail. The book includes descriptions of the participants, an index, and a short bibliography. Undergraduate students in business, community college and above.

GROWTH
INDUSTRIES
IN THE
1980s

New Titles from
QUORUM BOOKS

Danger: Marketing Researcher at Work
TERRY HALLER

OPEC, the Petroleum Industry, and United States Energy Policy
ARABINDA GHOSH

Corporate Internal Affairs: A Corporate and Securities Law Perspective
MARC I. STEINBERG

International Pharmaceutical Marketing
SURESH B. PRADHAN

Social Costs in Modern Society: A Qualitative and Quantitative Assessment
JOHN E. ULLMANN, EDITOR

Animal Law
DAVID S. FAVRE AND MURRAY LORING

Competing for Capital in the '80s: An Investor Relations Approach
BRUCE W. MARCUS

The International Law of Pollution: Protecting the Global Environment in a
World of Sovereign States
ALLEN L. SPRINGER

Statistical Concepts for Attorneys: A Reference Guide
WAYNE C. CURTIS

Handbook of Record Storage and Space Management
C. PETER WAEGEMANN

Industrial Bonds and the Rating Process
AHMED BELKAOUI

Of Foxes and Hen Houses: Licensing and the Health Professions
STANLEY J. GROSS

Telecommunications America: Markets Without Boundaries
MANLEY RUTHERFORD IRWIN

Pension Fund Investments in Real Estate: A Guide for Plan Sponsors and Real
Estate Professionals
NATALIE A. MCKELVY

GROWTH INDUSTRIES IN THE 1980s
Conference Proceedings

Sponsored by

Federal Reserve Bank of Atlanta

456659

Q
QUORUM BOOKS
Westport, Connecticut · London, England

Library of Congress Cataloging in Publication Data

Main entry under title:

Growth industries in the 1980s.

"Convened at the Atlanta Hilton Hotel in March
1983"—Pref.
Bibliography: p.
Includes index.
1. United States—Industries—Congresses. 2. United
States—Economic conditions—1981–   —Congresses.
3. Investments—United States—Congresses. 4. Economic
development—Congresses. I. Federal Reserve Bank of
Atlanta.
HC106.8.G76 1983   338.0973   83-13822
ISBN 0-89930-069-3 (lib. bdg.)

Library of Congress Catalog Card Number: 83-13822
ISBN: 0-89930-069-3

First published in 1983

Greenwood Press
A division of Congressional Information Service, Inc.
88 Post Road West
Westport, Connecticut 06881

Printed in the United States of America

10 9 8 7 6 5 4 3 2 1

Contents

Preface

What are the characteristics that permit some companies to grow and prosper while others languish? That question intrigued us at the Federal Reserve Bank of Atlanta and led to the "Growth Industries in the 1980s" conference and this book.

The question of corporate growth seemed particularly critical at the time our conference was convened at the Atlanta Hilton Hotel, in March 1983. Our nation had endured a long and trying recession that had left many businesses bankrupt and had left many states, including some in our Sixth Federal Reserve District, facing worrisome unemployment rates. Yet, over the past decade, this nation has added 15 million jobs to payrolls—more new jobs than the total employment of Canada, Sweden, and Switzerland combined. These new jobs, which have brought the number of Americans at work to more than 100 million, are attributable primarily to the energy and dynamic growth of our nation's small companies rather than to its corporate giants.

Looking beyond the painful though short-term slowdown that had afflicted the United States in 1981–1982, we knew that our nation was troubled by even more serious structural problems. Many of us, including Atlanta Fed President William F. Ford and Board Chairman William A. Fickling, Jr., were worried over our unimpressive economic growth, a mere shadow of the growth we had enjoyed in the 1960s, and the fact that we were being outdistanced by more aggressive global competitors. How could we, as a nation, encourage the companies and industries that can restore our competitive advantage? Faced with dilemmas of economic growth on both the short-term and long-term fronts, we concluded that the question was one that we, as a central bank, should address—and one whose deliberations should be recorded.

Our two-day conference drew more than 200 chief executive officers, financial planners, and journalists to hear the nation's leading thinkers on the subject of growth. Those who came represented a cross section of the industry within our six-state District. In addition, others came from as far away as California and England.

We feel that our visitors gained fresh insight into a timely question of critical importance. We hope that you, in reading this book, can share in that understanding. Obviously, the panelists' opinions recorded in the following chapters do not necessarily reflect those of the Atlanta Fed or the Federal Reserve System.

I would like to thank three people whose special, tireless efforts were invaluable in making the conference and this book possible—Gene Sullivan, Don Bedwell, and Carolyn Vincent.

Donald L. Koch
Senior Vice President and Research Director
Federal Reserve Bank of Atlanta

About the Contributors

James L. Bast became president of Dictaphone Corporation in January 1982 after serving as senior vice president, finance and administration, and chief financial officer of Dictaphone's parent company, Pitney Bowes Inc. A native of Baltimore, Bast began his career with Pitney Bowes in 1963 as a product research investigator. He worked for Bunker Ramo Corporation from 1972 to 1973 as division controller.

David T. Cook is Washington economics correspondent for *The Christian Science Monitor*. Cook has served as Detroit bureau chief and Chicago deputy bureau chief for McGraw-Hill News and as a correspondent for McGraw-Hill's *Business Week*. He was the recipient of a Walter Bagehot Fellowship in business journalism at Columbia University. He started his career as a journalist working in the *Monitor*'s Boston office.

William N. Cox, vice president and associate director of research at the Atlanta Fed, has responsibility for all research and public information products. He directs preparation of the monthly *Economic Review* and the semimonthly newsletter *Insight*. He also conducts and supervises research activities of the Research Department's eight research teams.

William A. Fickling, Jr., is chairman of Charter Medical Corporation, a Georgia-based company that owns and manages hospitals and health care facilities worldwide. He organized Charter Medical in 1969. Previously he worked as executive vice president of Fickling and Walker Inc. for seven years. A director of the Federal Reserve Bank of Atlanta since March 1978, he was designated as its chairman of the board in January 1980.

Malcolm S. Forbes, Jr., is president and chief operating officer of *Forbes*, one of the nation's oldest and most respected business publications. In addition to writing editorials for each issue of *Forbes*, he broadcasts economic commentaries for New York's public television. In both 1975 and 1976 he won the Crystal Owl, awarded each year to the reporter making the most accurate economic forecasts.

Walter A. Forbes serves as vice chairman and chief executive officer of Comp-U-Card of America Inc., a mail-order retailer based in Stamford, Connecticut. He is a former senior vice president of MAC Enterprises, the venture capital subsidiary of a faculty-based consulting firm headquartered in Cambridge, Massachusetts.

William F. Ford, as president of the Federal Reserve Bank of Atlanta, managed the Bank's activities in the Sixth Federal Reserve District. Before joining the Federal Reserve, he served as senior vice president in the Management Services Group at the Wells Fargo Bank in San Francisco, where he managed the economics department. Previously he was executive director of the American Bankers Association. He left the Atlanta Fed in October 1983 to become president of First Nationwide Financial Corporation in San Francisco.

W. Thomas J. Griffin is a founder and partner of G.T. Management Ltd., a London international investment management company with subsidiary offices in San Francisco, Hong Kong, Tokyo, and Australia. Before starting G.T. Management in 1969, he was managing director of a major group of closed-end investment trusts in London. He is a chartered accountant.

John T. Hartley, Jr., is president of Harris Corporation, a Melbourne, Florida, manufacturer of high-technology communication and information processing equipment. Hartley joined the company in 1956 as a research engineer in advanced development programs and business development. He taught at Auburn University, his alma mater, before joining Harris.

Howard R. Katz serves as president of Ocilla Industries, Inc., a southeast Georgia firm that produces manufactured housing. Ocilla's corporate headquarters are located in New York. He also has been controller of Estee Lauder, U.S.A., a major cosmetics manufacturer, and assistant to the executive vice president of C. Brewer & Company Limited, a diversified agricultural products and services company.

Donald L. Koch is senior vice president and director of research at the Federal Reserve Bank of Atlanta. He is the Bank's senior official responsible for economic research and public information. He also serves as associate economist to the Federal Open Market Committee when the Atlanta Bank's president is a voting member of the committee. Before joining the Reserve Bank in 1981, he had been an executive officer and corporate economist of Barnett Banks of Florida for eight years.

Arthur Levitt, Jr., has been chairman of the American Stock Exchange since leaving the presidency of the New York securities firm he helped found—Shearson/American Express. He is chairman and a founder of the American Business Conference, a Washington-based research and lobbying group for the nation's top growth companies. He is editor of *How to Make Your Money Make Money*, a compilation of investment advice from nineteen leading financial authorities.

Stephen A. Lieber is senior partner of Lieber & Co., investment advisors and members of the New York Stock Exchange. He is also president of the Evergreen Fund, the Evergreen Total Return Fund, and Saxon Woods Asset Management Corp. He was a partner of Vanden Broeck, Lieber & Co. from 1956 until 1969.

Edward J. Mathias is president of the T. Rowe Price New Horizons Fund, a no-load mutual fund concentrating on relatively small, rapidly growing companies. The New Horizons Fund held a portfolio in excess of $1.3 billion as of early 1983. His five years as a U.S. Navy Supply Corps officer before joining T. Rowe Price included a two-year sea duty assignment and a stint as a White House social aide.

Mancur Olson, a professor of economics at the University of Maryland, is the author of six books including *The Rise and Decline of Nations: Economic Growth, Stagflation, and Social Rigidities*. Olson has also written numerous articles. A Rhodes Scholar, he is a former deputy assistant secretary for the Department of Health, Education, and Welfare. He is immediate past president of the Southern Economic Association.

Thomas N. Roboz has been chairman of Stanwood Corporation, a Charlotte, North Carolina, apparel manufacturing firm, since 1968. Active in industry organizations, Roboz is past chairman or president of the American Apparel Manufacturers Association, the International Apparel Federation, and the U.S. Apparel Council. He has served as director of marketing for Willcox and Gibbs; chairman of the Opal Textilwerke in Hamburg, Germany; and president of the Apparel Corporation of America in Knoxville, Tennessee.

James Russell covers both national and regional business as financial editor of *The Miami Herald.* He writes a weekly investment column distributed to about 100 newspapers. During his 23 years with the *Herald* he also has served as business editor. Previously he worked as a correspondent, bureau chief, and regional editor in Atlanta for United Press International.

Richard Shaffer, *The Wall Street Journal*'s science and technology editor since 1981, guides the newspaper's coverage of medicine, science, and technology. Shaffer previously supervised the *Journal*'s technology column and worked as Boston bureau chief. He joined the *Journal* as a reporter in the Dallas bureau in 1970 after working for several southwestern newspapers, then was transferred to the New York bureau where he reported on the computer industry.

Ray Stevenson, a native of Columbus, Ohio, is president and a director of Charter Medical Corporation, a $400 million health care services company based in Macon, Georgia. Charter Medical owns, operates, manages, and develops hospitals in fifteen states, Saudi Arabia, London, and Puerto Rico. He joined Charter Medical in 1977 after serving as senior vice president for Hospital Affiliates International with responsibility for the company's pioneering work in the contract management of hospitals owned by others.

J. Leland Strange is president of Intelligent Systems Corporation of Norcross, Georgia, which manufactures color graphics computer equipment and personal computer enhancements. He was promoted to president of that firm in March 1983. Strange also serves as vice president of marketing for Quadram Corporation, a Norcross firm acquired by Intelligent Systems in 1982. He founded Quadram in 1981 with Tim Farris. Quadram manufactures and markets microcomputer enhancement products.

Gene D. Sullivan is research officer and leader of the regional economic research team at the Federal Reserve Bank of Atlanta. The native of Calamine, Arkansas, joined the Bank as an agricultural economist in 1969. He has been an associate professor at Louisiana State University, where he earned his master's and doctoral degrees in agricultural economics. He is co-author of the textbook *Economics: Applications to Agriculture and Agribusiness.*

Alvin Toffler, whose books include *Future Shock* and *The Third Wave,* is an author and social critic best known for his analyses of contemporary social change. Toffler's books have been published in 30 languages around the world. His work has won the McKinsey Foundation Book Award for "distinguished contribution to management literature." He holds five honorary degrees, serves on numerous boards, and is a member of the International Institute for Strategic Studies.

Robert H. Waterman, Jr., is co-author with Thomas J. Peters of the 1983 best-seller *In Search of Excellence: Lessons from America's Best-Run Companies.* He is a director of McKinsey & Co., Inc., where he is responsible for the firm's organization design and development program. Previously he helped open a Tokyo office and acted as managing director of McKinsey's Melbourne and Sydney, Australia, offices. He is a guest lecturer at Stanford University Graduate School of Business. Earlier he worked with IBM, the University of Denver Research Institute, and Marathon Oil Company.

John H. Weitnauer, Jr., is deputy chairman of the Atlanta Fed's board of directors. He has been chairman of Richway, a division of Federated Department Stores, Inc., since March 1980. Prior to that he was president of Richway and executive vice president of Rich's, the parent company of Richway. Since starting with Rich's in 1956 as a divisional service superintendent he has been general manager of two Rich's branch stores, vice president of personnel, and executive vice president.

WILLIAM A. FICKLING, JR.

Introductory Remarks

I'm encouraged by the interest we are seeing in "Growth Industries in the 1980s," considering that a recession has forced a lot of firms to retrench rather than expand.

Let's hope we are addressing this question at a time when our economy is moving into a more upbeat phase that will bring greater prosperity for the firms within our Sixth Federal Reserve District and across the nation. And let's hope that the newfound prosperity will trigger more aggressive expansion by those firms.

Some may find it unusual for a central bank to be sponsoring a forum such as this, but the Federal Reserve Bank of Atlanta takes a broad view of its mission. In addition to traditional central banking responsibilities such as processing checks, coins, and currency, a Reserve Bank should monitor the pulse of its District's economy. Our staff of economists and the business people who serve as directors on various Atlanta Fed boards help keep our president briefed on economic developments in the six states within the District we serve as a central bank. That grass-roots input helps guide the Federal Reserve's conduct of national monetary policy.

As an outgrowth of the Atlanta Fed's economic research activities, this Bank, under President William Ford, has emerged as a major forum for significant economic questions. Those include questions that are important not only to the financial institutions in the Sixth District, but to the broader business community as well. The Atlanta Fed staged its first major conferences in June 1981. In fact, it started off in a big way, with a double-header—first, a conference on "The Future of the Financial Services Industry," followed a couple of weeks later by a conference on "The Future of the U.S. Payments System."

After directing those two conferences at the financial services industry, the Bank looked beyond financial services in March 1982 with a conference on "Supply-Side Economics in the 1980s." That gathering was cosponsored by Emory University's Law and Economics Center. It featured some of the Reagan administration's chief economic spokes-men, two Nobel prize-winners in economics, three congressmen, and some of the nation's leading scholars in supply-side theory.

This discussion should prove a worthy successor to the supply-side gathering, and one that will broaden all of our perspectives still further. Like the supply-side meeting, our conference on growth industries was put together by the Atlanta Fed's Research Department under Donald L. Koch, senior vice president and director of research. Under Don, the Research Department has focused an increasing amount of attention on our region, its financial institutions, and its other industries.

WILLIAM F. FORD

Conference Purpose and Overview

William Fickling has noted that we have endured a rather long and trying recession, one that only now appears to be fading. It seems significant that some firms have managed to succeed even in troubled times, while others have been bemoaning their fate. That raises an interesting question: How is it that some firms seem to be able to prosper and grow rapidly, both in good times and in bad times?

It was during some of the gloomiest months of the recession that we began to direct our attention toward this question at the Atlanta Fed. We also began to wonder what specific characteristics highly successful companies share.

How do they do it? Some people used to say that all it took was a location in the booming Sunbelt, and a corporation had it made. Tell that to some of the steel companies around Birmingham, or to the home builders in South Florida—or to some of the struggling textile and forest products firms in Georgia. Others asserted that a unique market can guarantee profitability, or that an innovative product line can turn the trick.

Does size help provide additional momentum for growth? Some might argue that a company gains strength as it grows. Certainly, size can generate vast revenues or can help a firm underwrite expansion into new ventures or new markets. Others have said that a more compact firm, blessed with greater flexibility, holds a competitive edge if it knows how to exploit it. There's no question that certain small firms have been able to run circles around bigger competitors that have grown too unwieldy to respond to changing markets.

What about differences in corporate structure and organization? Is the tightly centralized firm the most efficient and productive? Or should a management emphasize a looser, more independent organization with relatively autonomous operating units? Should executives ignore traditional departmental boundaries to create "adhocracies" to deal with problems, task-force style, as they emerge?

Most critical of all, we'll look at the importance of extraordinary management. Can a superior management compete successfully against firms that enjoy other advantages? Some of our experts will explore that element in depth.

We will lead off with a session on key growth characteristics—a session that will begin with Professor Mancur Olson, speaking on the environment for growth. Next will be Arthur Levitt, Jr., chairman of the American Stock Exchange, focusing on the importance of growth. He will offer his perspective from a major stock exchange where investors buy and sell shares in some of our nation's fastest growing companies. Levitt will be followed by a panel of securities experts who will discuss the elements that sophisticated investors look for in a growth company.

That will lead us up to Robert H. Waterman, Jr., whose research into corporate success led to the best-selling book *In Search of Excellence*. His presentation, like the book he co-authored, should provide new insight into the factors that inspire greatness in premier growth companies. Waterman will share his thoughts on corporate traits ranging from risk taking to organizational structure and the "ownership" that employees feel they have in a growth company and its decisions.

Session II is titled "Industries to Accommodate an Expanding Population." It will include presentations on computerized retailing, medical services, and housing. Session III, "Emerging Growth Industries," will feature presentations on some of the nation's fastest growing high-tech industries: electronics, telecommunications, and automated office equipment.

Next in line will be Alvin Toffler, social critic and the author of several books including *Future Shock* and *The Third Wave*. In his books, Toffler has introduced us to an evolving Third Wave of civilization which he says is supplanting our Second Wave industrial age—which in its day replaced a First Wave society based on agriculture. His topic is "Toward a Third Wave Economy"—and he clearly has been out front in identifying trends that will shape the future.

He'll be followed by a session on "Growth Prospects for Traditional Industries," focusing on industries such as textiles and apparel that have provided jobs in this country since the Industrial Revolution—but which now must respond to change or lose their markets to foreign competitors. Then we will present four respected business journalists offering their perspectives on the whole exciting subject of growth.

Now, let's get started with Donald L. Koch, our director of research.

I. KEY GROWTH CHARACTERISTICS

Donald L. Koch, Moderator

Before we begin this discussion of key growth characteristics, let me explain why we believe that this is a crucial subject for our country.

Our nation's economy, as you know, is growing at very marginal rates. At such a time, it is vital in terms of national policy that we learn to identify and to stimulate the sectors with the potential to provide the largest share of jobs and to make the greatest contribution to GNP.

How do we, as a nation, identify and encourage the high-performance sectors likely to contribute significantly to our national economic health? How do we gain a better understanding of the dimensions of our growth, so we can better respond to it? How do we direct our growth? Do we adopt some variant of the Japanese approach, which includes rewarding the winners and discouraging the prospective losers? Does it make sense, from either an economic or a social standpoint, to subsidize failing industries that might better be allowed to die in peace?

Leading off will be Mancur Olson, a professor of economics at the University of Maryland, discussing "The Ideal Environment for Nurturing Growth." I imagine he will touch on all of the environmental elements that can inspire, or discourage, growth—cultural, governmental, political, even social.

Olson has conducted some revealing comparisons of the various regions of our country. He has looked closely at the `South, for instance, and the unique set of circumstances that fostered this region's emergence after World War II.

Our second presentation will be offered by Arthur Levitt, Jr., chairman of the American Stock Exchange and a leading spokesman for growth companies as chairman of the American Business Conference, a research and lobbying group he helped to organize. He will discuss the importance of growth, from his unique vantage point on the subject.

Levitt will be followed by a panel discussion on "What the Investor Looks For," featuring some of the most respected men in the securities and investment field. Our panelists include Edward J. Mathias, president of the T. Rowe Price New Horizons Fund; Stephen A. Lieber, president of the Evergreen Fund; and W. Thomas J. Griffin, a founder and partner of England's G.T. Management Ltd.

Those experts will discuss the elements that investment banking firms look for in a company. Do they look for size? Are growth and earnings the crucial factors? Is it a proprietary product? Is it an unregulated industry, unrestrained by federal or local government red tape? We'll see.

MANCUR OLSON

The Ideal Environment for Nurturing Growth

I saw an ad from Pan American World Airways recently, emphasizing that Pan American was the world's most experienced airline. Of course, that's a reassuring thought, because none of us likes to fly with a pilot who hasn't had any practice. But I was thinking that it's amazing how many of the experienced old airlines are now having financial trouble and some are even in danger of bankruptcy.

Then I saw an ad for Piedmont Airlines that claimed it is doing very well indeed, growing and making profits. Piedmont said the big airlines shouldn't look back because it is gaining on them. Then I thought of other regional and new airlines, like Peoples Airline, for example, which are doing relatively well.

And it occurred to me, isn't it amazing that some of the new inexperienced airlines—or some of the small ones confined to smaller markets—seemed to be doing reasonably well, while some of the most experienced and largest seemed to be doing badly?

Suppose we look at the United States economy today and ask, for example, what are some of our most experienced industries in American manufacturing? Well, we could say that the steel industry is certainly an experienced industry in this country. We were first in automobiles historically, and our automobile industry is certainly experienced. We are rather experienced in farm machinery also. Perhaps only our textile and railroad industries are older.

The list of industries I've just mentioned doesn't make you want to cheer at the moment, does it? Steel, God knows, is doing badly enough in this country. No one needs to be told about what's happening to our automobile industry nor of the dangers facing International Harvester right now. And I can't imagine anyone who is terribly likely to make exalted statements about our railroad or textile industries.

By contrast, some less experienced industries, like many of our high technology industries, are on average doing better. Again, since practice obviously helps and there's plainly something in the idea that experience teaches you something, this is maybe a bit puzzling.

Suppose we now switch from firms and industries to regions and countries. Let's ask which are the most experienced regions and countries when it comes to modern industry and modern economic life.

Of all the countries in the world, beyond any doubt, the most experienced in industry and manufacturing is Great Britain. It is the country of the Industrial Revolution starting in about 1760, and the country which, until at least the middle of the nineteenth century, was indisputably the industrial and economic leader of the world. But it hasn't been doing so well lately, and everyone, I'm sure, has heard of the "British disease"—the tendency for that economy to behave in a fashion the British tend to describe as sick.

Now suppose we ask, What are the most experienced regions within our own country, particularly the most experienced in manufacturing? Quite obviously, it's the industrial Northeast and older Middle West, the areas where industry has existed longest.

The West, more recently settled, and the South, industrialized extensively only after World War II, are clearly less experienced. Yet, again, what do we see? The Northeast and the older Middle West are relatively depressed. The newer South and West are doing relatively better. Again, it is the opposite of what we would expect by looking at the value of experience.

Now let's look at some other countries since World War II, for example, Japan and Germany, Korea, and Taiwan. We find that these countries—especially Germany just after the war, and Japan, Taiwan, and Korea in the 1960s—grew at rates that were regarded as fantastic; people spoke, for example, of the economic miracles in these countries.

Of course, people wouldn't call something a miracle unless it were outside of normal experience and explanation in terms of familiar laws and principles. But, after World War II, Germany and Japan were essentially starting from scratch. Maybe they weren't completely inexperienced, but they were certainly less experienced and at a disadvantage, it would seem, compared with countries like Britain and the United States. Yet they did much better, while utterly inexperienced Korea and Taiwan did better still.

So we've seen a whole series of examples of firms and industries and countries and regions where the inexperienced do better than the experienced. Since practice clearly is valuable, how can this be true? Is there something in economics, as there is in romance, where the virgins have an advantage? I think there is.

I've been thinking about this for some time now and I've just written a book on that topic, called *The Rise and Decline of Nations* (Yale University Press, 1982). I'd like to go into one very small part of that book at the moment, because I believe its findings will relate to the problems and opportunities Americans, and especially American businessmen, confront today.

Now, I start in an unusual place for books in economics. I start by looking at associations or organizations or combinations that operate in the political system to lobby the government, or that combine or organize in the market to influence some price or wage—to get a higher, cartelistic price by selling less.

These lobbying and cartelizing associations or collusions all have in common one feature that has been overlooked until lately, but which seems to me terribly, terribly important: that any such organization provides to its clients a benefit or service that goes automatically to everyone in some category or group. Let's take the lobbying organization first.

Any time a lobbying organization lobbies for a tariff or a subsidy or a tax loophole, that tariff or subsidy or tax loophole goes to every individual or firm in an industry or category whether or not it helped support the lobby that won the special favor.

Now consider cartels. Suppose some of the OPEC oil producers sell less oil in order to push up its price. That high price will then be available to any producer of oil whether or not that producer restricted its own output and contributed to the reduction in output that raised the price.

Analytically speaking, the good provided by either a lobby or a cartel-type organization, because it goes to everyone in some category, is a "collective" or "public good." It is rather like the basic services provided by government, such as law and order and defense, which also go to everyone in some group or country. But we know governments need taxes to support themselves because governments obviously can't sell services like law and order and defense in a market.

How, then, can the organizations that lobby or cartelize support themselves given that their services, too, are not generally marketable?

I found in looking at these organizations that, if they are large and if they last any length of time, they always have some gimmick that accounts for their membership. These gimmicks, which I call "selective incentives," account for their membership, rather than the basic services that they provide, which would go to people whether they joined or not.

For example, the simplest and most obvious case is the union shop and the picket line for labor unions. Quite clearly, here's a case where membership is compulsory or nearly so. This compulsion is mainly what explains the union's membership because, of course, an individual worker would get the higher wage any union wins whether or not he or she personally was paying dues or out there on the picket line contributing to a strike.

The union example is just the simplest and most conspicuous of a whole array of such devices that induce individuals and firms to join organizations that provide collective goods for their group or category. Semi-coercive and coercive measures—social pressure and things like that—are very important to professional associations, for example.

Similarly, farm organization membership often is explained by the fact that the organizations are tied in with farm cooperatives and mutual insurance companies. The farm organizations' dues, like those of the Farmers' Union and the Farm Bureau, are often taken out of the patronage dividends that come from patronizing the farm cooperative. That's what accounts largely for the membership in the farm organizations.

Small organizations, however, sometimes can organize without these special selective incentives or gimmicks. Each member may get a sufficient part of the benefit in a small group so that you may get some voluntary cooperation for the good of the group.

Now you may say, "Oh, this sounds very different from old age and experience. What's this got to do with what you started to talk about, Olson?" It has a lot to do with it. The difficulties of collective action, and particularly of getting a lobbying or cartelizing organization started, tell us something about how long it will take before such organizations can become important.

If getting collective action to lobby or cartelize is difficult and problematical because these organizations provide collective goods, then we have to ask how and when will these organizations get going, *if* they succeed in getting going.

I would argue that such organizations get going only when they've got unusually good leadership and only when there are also favorable circumstances.

I am reminded of the example of Jimmy Hoffa when he was a teenager working in a warehouse. One hot June day a large shipment of fresh strawberries came in. These fresh strawberries would soon spoil and had to be gotten out to the retailers and to the customers quickly.

But young Jimmy Hoffa, cunning and courageous as he was, chose that moment to organize a strike and a union. The employer gave in rather than lose the fresh strawberries.

Now my argument is that any given group is going to have the able leadership—the Jimmy Hoffa—and the lucky circumstances—the fresh strawberries—only in the fullness of time. If we have a stable society that over a long period is spared the violence or repression that destroys organizations, then we have a society that gradually will accumulate more and more organizations to lobby or cartelize. That is because the more time that passes, the larger the number of groups that will have had the good leadership and luck needed to get organized.

So stable societies or regions will accumulate more of these organizations as time goes on. That is also true of industries and firms that are more experienced and have more history behind them.

Now you say, all right, but so what? What difference does this make? We can see the difference it makes if we look at it this way: Given that a group or an association is organized to lobby or to cartelize, what incentives will it have? Will it have an incentive to make the society more productive or less productive? We can best understand this, I think, by looking for a moment at an association that we will say, arbitrarily, represents 1 percent of the country. Let's say we're talking about a labor union whose members represent 1 percent of the population. Or we're talking about a business association whose members in the aggregate own capital that earns 1 percent of the national income, or a professional association of similar size.

Let's now ask what such an organization could do that would best serve the interests of its members or clients. Could it, for example, make its members or clients better off by making the country or region in which that association existed better off?

In general, it is better to be part of a prosperous and efficient country than of a poor and inefficient one. Presumably, all associations are sincere in wanting the best for the country of which they are a part. But will a lobbying or cartelistic organization that represents 1 percent of the country serve its members best by trying to make the country in which its members live more productive?

Remember my assumption that the organization represents 1 percent of the country. We immediately see that if this lobbying association works to make the country more efficient, say by getting inefficient legislation repealed or efficient legislation passed, it will bear the whole cost of the effort. Yet the members will get only 1 percent of the benefit that comes from making the country more prosperous. That is to say that, on average, if the national income goes up by $1 million, this group will get 1 percent of that.

So we see that only in the most exceptional circumstances could it pay such an association to try to make its society better off. The cost-benefit ratio of actions to make the society better off would have to be 100 to 1 or better for such an association to find it advantageous to use its resources that way.

But how then could the association make its members better off? Well, if it could get a larger slice of the national output for its own membership, then its members would be made better off by that.

But, you may say, if we have distributional struggle—if we have a lobby winning special-interest legislation or if we have a cartel-type organization selling less and charging more for it—then that special-interest legislation or that cartelization will make the economy less efficient. The economy will produce less, so the pie will shrink. As the group gets a larger slice of the social pie, the pie will get smaller.

Note that if we're talking about a group that is 1 percent of the size of the country, then, it will suffer, on average, 1 percent of the loss that comes from the shrinkage of the pie, yet get all of the larger slice.

In other words, this association that lobbies or cartelizes will make its membership better off by distributional struggle that gives its members a larger slice of the social output, even if the costs to the society are up to 100 times as great as the amount redistributed to this group.

So these groups' incentives are not to produce but to engage in distributional struggle and to persevere in these distributional struggles, even if the social costs are a gigantic multiple of the amount they win.

Thus the right analogy really is not the slicing of the pie; it's more like wrestlers battling over the contents of a china shop and breaking more than they carry away.

There is a test to see whether what I'm saying gives us any insight into the major economic realities of our time. That test is to see whether the older and more experienced nations, regions, industries, and firms, despite the advantages of their greater experience, are usually doing worse than most people expected.

You recall that I started with the most experienced of the industrial countries, Great Britain. No country has had such a long time to accumulate special-interest organizations, and no major developed democracy is growing more slowly than Great Britain. It has suffered from the "British disease" under the left wing and right wing governments alike.

The relatively slow British growth started in the laissez-faire period in the late nineteenth century. But this slow growth couldn't possibly be due to any permanent change in the British culture or people. Remember, it was the British who discovered rapid economic growth with their industrial revolution of the eighteenth century.

If we look at our own country, we again see that the regions that have had the longest time of industrialization and the longest time to accumulate special-interest organization have experienced the slowest growth. These parts of the country also have the highest level of membership in special-interest organizations. The West, more recently settled, has had less time to accumulate such organizations, and so has the defeated and, until lately, turbulent South. And, as you know, the West and the South lately have proved to be better environments for economic growth.

Similarly, if the logic I've put forth is right, what should we have expected when totalitarian governments like those of Hitler and Tojo swept the slate clean of special-interest organizations in Germany and Japan? We would expect that, after these regimes were toppled and a free and stable legal order generally favorable to economic growth was established, these countries would grow faster than others with similar legal frameworks. Of course, Germany and Japan have grown with exceptional rapidity. So have Japan's former colonies of Korea and Taiwan.

Now let's look at experienced versus less experienced industries. My colleague, Peter Murrell, reacting to an early draft of my argument, decided that he would look at old versus new industries in West Germany and Britain. He reasoned that an old industry is more likely to have accumulated special-interest organization than a young industry. The managers will have had more time to work out some kind of lobby or collusion for price fixing, the workers more time to form a union, and so on. By contrast, even in a long-stable country like Great Britain, a brand new industry or a brand new firm in a new line of activity won't have had much time to accumulate special-interest organization.

Murrell accordingly hypothesized that, while we would expect industry in general to be doing better in West Germany than in Britain, new industries in Britain should be less behind new industries in West Germany than old industries were. To test this hypothesis, he took the ratios of the growth rates of new to old British industries and compared them with the ratios of the growth rates of new to old industries in West Germany. He found that, relatively speaking, the new industries did better in Britain than in Germany. New British industries did much better in relationship to old British industries than new West German industries did in relation to old West German industries.

We can see a similar pattern in airlines, or steel companies, or automobile companies in the United States. Let's look at an old airline company in a regulated industry where the permission of a regulatory authority was needed for a new airline to enter. Since regulatory authorities are much influenced by the firms they regulate, naturally the authorities were not hospitable to new entrants. We might ask what we would expect to happen to an airline that was accumulating experience over a long time and doing so in a regulated environment.

Well, the regulators are going to see that the organizations don't lose money in the long run. That means if the costs of the airlines go up, then prices have to be raised so the organization doesn't lose money.

So if there won't be losses even though costs go up, what incentive do the inputs, which are the source of the costs, have? They have an incentive to ask for more in the way of pay and to offer less in the way of work.

The managers in these companies have an incentive to expect higher pay, easier work, thicker carpets, more corporate jets, and all the other perquisites of the easy life. And the workers have an incentive to seek more and more in the way of wages, for less and less in the way of work.

So pilots in the experienced airlines frequently earn much more than $100,000 a year, even when equally skilled pilots would be available in the free market for, say, $30,000 or $40,000. Admittedly, the regulated environment for airlines and railways is perhaps more than typically favorable to my case. But let's think now of the unregulated steel, automobile, and farm machinery industries. What happened there? Well, until the antitrust laws stopped it in the steel industry, we had the "Pittsburgh plus" method of pricing and eventually very strong unionization through the United Steel Workers. In automobiles and farm machinery, there were similar patterns of oligopolistic concentration and heavy unionization.

And these are among the areas experiencing import competition. In steel and automobiles, for example, we're having to import disproportionately because countries less experienced at making steel and countries less experienced at making automobiles are outdoing us. This is exactly what the theory I've put forth in *The Rise and Decline of Nations* would lead us to expect.

There's a message or two here for the businessman. One of these is illustrated by Pan American's decision to buy National a while back in order to get an airline with a set of domestic routes and experience in serving the domestic market. Pan American bought National at just about the time deregulation was taking place. In doing this, it bought not only some experience but also the accumulation of those excess costs that emerge in firms protected by lobbying and cartelization. In this case, the cartelization had been enforced by the system of governmental regulation.

I would like to suggest in general that if you are a banker asking to whom you should lend, you should remember that experience is important because practice does help. But you've also got to ask, What over time has been accumulated besides experience that's built into that cost structure? Sometimes the less experienced firm that may appear to be a less worthy credit prospect has in fact a much brighter future.

The logic I've put forth can explain many, many other things. But there is only time enough now to go into how it explains the recession that we've all been suffering through, especially in 1982.

How can we explain why, in our society and some other societies, some years are recession and depression years, whereas others are exceptionally good, or boom years?

By my argument, societies age over time. But if they age at a regular rate, then why should some years be especially bad and others especially good? If a boom follows a recession, how can that boom be explained, given that after the recession the society and the relevant industries are only a year or so older?

The secret has to do with the way the associations I've been discussing make decisions. And alas, this matter has been neglected in all of the macroeconomic theories. Keynesian theory, monetarist theory, and the new equilibrium macroeconomics have all neglected this matter, and that's one reason why we have been in such a fix in the last couple of years.

The key to the matter, as I claim to show in *The Rise and Decline of Nations*, is that groups cannot make decisions as quickly as individuals. We've all been part of committee meetings that take a long time to come to a decision. We've probably even been part of committee meetings that take a long time *not* to come to a decision.

So a group of firms will make decisions less quickly than a single firm and a group of individuals will make decisions less quickly than a single individual. One reason for this is the by-laws and democratic procedures in larger organizations. Elections are conducted every so often, meetings are held every so often, and notice has to be given of meetings. Major decisions, then, can take place only after a certain amount of time has passed. So groups that have to follow democratic procedures take time to make decisions.

Similarly, groups that bargain with one another and make decisions unanimously by voluntary agreement also take some time to make decisions. Suppose we take a group of oligopolistic firms that are trying to fix prices and block entry in some industry. In general, if all of the firms but one agree to restrict output and raise the price, that won't do the trick because the one firm that didn't agree can take advantage of the higher price brought about by the reduced sales of the others. The cartel breaker can expand its own sales and get the whole advantage of the other firms' output restriction.

In general, then, unless there are special cost conditions, unanimous consent is needed. But to get unanimous agreement can take some time, especially as it is rational in the bargaining for individual parties to be holdouts—to demand a better deal as a condition of their participation.

So slow decision-making is typical of the special-interest groups of which I speak. This is one reason they are not good for innovation, because it takes them a long time to agree on things like new technologies. It took a long time, for example, before the labor savings of the diesel locomotive were realized. That's true even though all parties could have been better off by saving the extra man and dividing up the gains from that saving among all the participants, including those who had been firemen on the old steam locomotives.

This slow decision-making is also terribly important in a way that Keynes and Friedman and all the other great macro theorists have overlooked: When agreement on prices or wages is required because of collusion, or when by-laws have to be followed because there's a formal organization, then we have slow decision-making on prices and wages.

Any group, even a powerful cartel or a group that has enough lobbying power to make the government set a price for it, cannot sell as much if it raises prices. Even such a group must consider that, as you raise prices more and more, eventually sales fall off to such a point that it isn't in your interest to raise the price any more, however complete the monopoly power of your group. All demand curves—at least income-compensated demand curves—are downward sloping.

Every group, however powerful, must choose a price or wage that's best for it. That price or wage will always be much higher than the competitive price or wage but, of course, it won't be infinitely high. Taking into account the situation as it sees it, a group, by its slow decision-making procedures, agrees on a price or a wage that seems best for it: a price or wage that's higher than the competitive one, but not so high that it cripples sales. In general, these prices and wages are set in nominal terms; that is to say, they are set in terms of money.

Suppose, then, we have a cartel-type organization or lobbying-type organization setting some price or wage at so many dollars per unit or so many dollars per hour. Let us suppose that there is unexpected inflation so that after this particular price is set, prices rise in the economy in general. Because of inflation, this price or wage that we are talking about is now lower relative to other prices or wages than this organization desired.

The organization will then want to raise its price to take the inflation into account and to obtain the same real or relative price it had planned on initially. But that's going to take some time, often quite some time. Labor-management agreements in this country, for example, normally last for three years.

So, during periods of unexpected inflation, the prices set by the combinations with lobbies or monopoly powers are lower in real or relative terms than they would otherwise be. The losses from monopoly are accordingly also less than they would otherwise be, and unemployment is lower as well. Not only unemployment of labor but unemployment of other resources is also less than it would otherwise be because these monopoly prices are, in real terms, lower than the organizations that set them wanted them to be.

Thus, for a while unexpected inflation is associated with better times. Of course, it won't do to inflate permanently; permanent inflation comes to be expected, and this is taken into account in the price and wage setting. But a one-time unexpected inflation will have the effects I've described.

Now let us suppose we have a different situation. Let's suppose no one believes that inflation is going to be lowered by much or that the monetary policy will be very tough. Suppose, for whatever reason, that for a time there is less inflation than was expected.

This was true in 1982. Not long ago, at a meeting organized by a bank in my area near Washington, the bank reported the results of a poll that had been taken at the corresponding meeting a year before. Practically everyone present at the meeting a year earlier had predicted a higher rate of inflation than actually materialized.

What happened in 1982 is that the inflation rate was lower than most people had expected a year or two earlier. But that means that any cartel or lobbying-type organization setting prices a year or two before, expecting more inflation than actually occurred, set a higher price in money terms that turned out to be higher in real terms than it wanted. Thus the special-interest organizations' prices or wages were even higher than was in their members' interests. The losses from monopoly, then, are greater than normal and the unemployment is greater than normal when there is unexpected deflation or disinflation because firms and workers are priced out of the market.

Many people talk about "core" inflation, but they don't explain what is at the core of any proper theory of stagflation and recession: the slow decision-making of special-interest groups.

So, tying it all together, we must conclude that not only in human life and in the life of animals, but also in firms, industries, regions, and nations, there is, alas, an aging process. Perhaps a better analogy to this institutional aging process is the aging of wine or the aging of cheese or the aging of a mountain range. Nothing can remain the same as time goes on. Our heretofore somewhat timeless, undynamic, static economic theory has left this out. But we cannot solve the problems of our country, our region, our industries, or our firms unless we take it into account.

ARTHUR LEVITT, JR.

Why Growth Is Important

Any attempt to explain the importance of economic growth invites the easy rhetoric of the rising tide lifting all boats and the magic of our free market system. The platitudes, however, have little cogency at the Federal Reserve Bank of Atlanta, so let's proceed with the premise that I assume is acceptable to even the cynics among us: that after a prolonged and painful period of stagnation, the importance of growth has never been clearer. Simply stated, growth is the key to America's future prosperity and America's future competitiveness.

Cardinal Newman once suggested that growth is the only evidence of life. In economic terms, we might wish to amend Cardinal Newman's definition to state that growth in many of its facets is the best insurance against an untimely demise. To understand the fundamental importance of growth and to stay away from the cliches, we must try to identify the kind of growth that works best for America.

Growth for its own sake is clearly preferable to no growth, but growth for its own sake is also the ideology of the cancer cell. The economic landscape is littered with the burned-out hulks of companies that made a blind commitment to the concept of growth and then proved unable to cope with its consequences.

In the international arena, we see major third world nations such as Mexico and Brazil suddenly face-to-face with potential disaster. Why? Because they experienced strong but unstructured growth that left them overextended and unable to adapt to changing economic circumstances.

On the other side of the ledger, we can see that companies and nations that have planned for growth wisely, using it as a lever to increase productivity and income, are the economic success stories of the past decade.

By wisely, I don't mean the total central control that reaches its extreme in the failed economies of communist nations. I mean, rather, the achievement of a social consensus that allows for a cooperative effort to reach broad, agreed-upon goals.

As Wassily Leontief, New York University Nobel Prize winner for economics, so lucidly put it: "National selection in modern society is very expensive. We could build 20 new industries and wait around to see which might succeed, but should we? Even in nature, creatures find a way to cooperate and survive. Look at the beaver. Beavers work together; beavers don't build dams that don't work. In man, that is called planning."

Now the kind of growth that provides new jobs and a rising standard of living for a society occurs when output rises faster than the number of jobs. That is real growth as opposed to the mere expansion that is cloaked in the password of growth. It has subtle but extremely important advantages. Real growth blazes a trail for the flow of labor and resources into the most efficient and productive sectors of an economy. It emphasizes strength and facilitates adjustment to change.

These days, it's difficult to overstate the importance of the ability to adapt to change. Let me give you an example. Clive Sinclair, the British genius who invented the inexpensive personal computer and who has often been correct in the past, offers the prediction that the 1990s will differ from the 1970s as profoundly as the nineteenth century differed from the eighteenth.

Sinclair sees a century of change telescoped into a decade—this decade—with society on the verge of dramatic transformations in which manufacturing jobs will virtually disappear in countries like ours as we turn from products of the material to products of the mind.

Even if his view is extreme, there is no denying that we are living in the midst of rapid and profound change, revolutionary change, a mile-a-minute change where no nation, no growth company, can afford to fall behind the power curve and still remain competitive.

Just as growing and dynamic economies and companies thrive on change and turn it to their advantage, stagnant ones tend to play it close to the vest and cling to the status quo. But real growth leads to the optimum allocation of resources, which makes for tough competition, whether it's a company or a country. That is precisely why we see growing nations dominating new markets while their less successful competitors erect barriers that they hope will protect them from an inability to compete.

There was a time in this nation when it was really fashionable to be against growth. It was a standard borne mostly by those who already had their share of the American dream and wanted to pull up the drawbridge. Now, after years of inflation, stagflation, stagnation, and recession, I guess we are not hearing too much about that notion any more.

Growth is looking better and better. Perhaps that is why there is such a vast demand for policies and priorities that are intended to produce sustained real growth and build a more prosperous future for this nation.

Now one would think that after all these years of economic turmoil and crises, we might have learned that it is very tough to solve economic challenges like growth with mirrors and nostrums. Yet the notion persists that if we can just find the single right gimmick—if we can learn from the Japanese who seem to do everything right—perhaps we could turn things around in America.

Maybe that is why we hear so much these days about an American industrial policy. Sometimes it seems that every economist and politician is trying to promote his or her own special brand of national economic planning.

Now at one end of the spectrum, we have a talented, innovative leader such as Felix Rohatyn who wants the federal government to recapture the spirit of the New Deal—to decide the nature and the future of our basic industries, to determine how they can be modernized to meet the goals set for them, and to raise the capital essential to meet these objectives. Rohatyn is talking about a multibillion-dollar Reconstruction Finance Corporation and powers that have not been voluntarily ceded to the government for a number of generations.

I'm not suggesting that America has ceased to need basic industries or that we should turn our backs on smokestack companies in favor of high technology. We were founded to be a just and compassionate society. We have an overriding obligation to remain one.

Thus, while we can't afford to cling tenaciously to the past, we can certainly help our people to retrain and adjust to the future. We can encourage the process of technological change that will gradually reshape, revitalize, and even redirect our smokestack industries.

Nevertheless, the concept of an expensive, active, interventionist policy to rescue and revive ailing basic industries, such as steel, poses a number of very serious questions as to whether such policies really do contribute to growth.

An industry such as steel has problems that transcend the availability of capital and the cost of labor. The weight of the average American car, for example, has been decreased by 1,000 pounds in just a few years. Countries such as Korea, Brazil, and many others have competitive advantages in producing steel that would cause us real problems even in a world of perfectly free trade.

Another problem with the Rohatyn approach to industrial policy is that once a basic industry is identified and targeted for salvation, there are going to be inevitable calls from all over the country, from every part of the political spectrum, to protect it. We'll be hearing the old infant industries' argument. Once that kind of "temporary" protection is put in place, I think you know that it tends to stay on the books forever, distorting patterns of trade and inhibiting resources from moving to where they can be used most productively.

The flip side of Rohatyn's basic industry strategy for growth is Lester Thurow's proposal to use government intervention on the Japanese model to accelerate the development of so-called New Horizon industries. Thurow wants to shift resources to expanding sectors of the economy, silicon chips, laser optics, and synthetics. He wants to locate and force-feed the IBMs and Xeroxes of the future and to simply beat our competitors with the new technology.

I wish him luck. As the chief executive officer of a major stock exchange just filled with high-growth companies, I have spent most of my adult life watching the best experts in the business community try to pick the winners. One thing I have learned is there simply is no formula for success, no guidelines that can be issued to bureaucrats in Washington so they are able to spot tomorrow's winner. Literally thousands of promising well-managed firms are stretched all across this country, but if anyone can tell me how to pick the next Hewlett-Packard, I have a place for him or her on our payroll.

I submit it is almost impossible to make judgments as to which industry or technology is now in a state of decline or a state of ascendency or obsolescence and thereby deserves federal assistance. Also, who is to determine at what stage in the decline of an industry it is appropriate to pull the plug?

American economic history is absolutely replete with examples of industries that appeared to be obsolete, only to achieve Phoenix-like resurrection. The American petroleum industry has gone through a number of such metamorphoses: first after the invention of the electric light bulb, and second after the invention of space heating in the 1920s, followed by the enormous resurgence of demand during World War II.

On the other side of the coin, our national infatuation with wonder products and industries has often missed the mark or significantly underestimated the time it might take to realize their potential. Biotech is a prime example. The infusion of massive amounts of government capital a few years ago, when biotech seemed to be the password for the future, would have been an economic catastrophe.

When we talk about picking winners, let's also remember that we live in a democracy. This second industrial revolution differs from its nineteenth-century predecessor in one important respect: The victims of the technological revolution today are not politically powerless. The unemployed exist in larger numbers and they're often much better organized. When people were displaced from farms in an earlier time, manufacturing absorbed them. Now we are asking too much to expect high technology alone to put everyone to work. We must foster growth in many segments of the economy, such as services, foods, even toys.

There's going to be a political aspect to any industrial policy that attempts to target winners and heaps rewards on a few selected industries in a few lucky districts. The more political the process of encouraging growth becomes, the more I suggest it will fail economically.

Those are just two examples from the shopping list of industrial policies available to America. Between Thurow and Rohatyn there is a broad spectrum of proposals, but they all seem to have two points in common. First, they all agree that America should have an industrial policy. Second, they share a commitment to growth and competitiveness.

At the opposite extreme, it's tempting to oppose any industrial policy at all. But it's also futile, because America already has a policy of sorts. It's ad hoc. It's haphazard. It's the product of thousands of interventions every day, every hour, virtually every minute. We see public-sector interventions in the private sector, in agriculture, in ship building, in defense, in regulations, in trigger pricing, even in such things as labeling and pollution standards.

But if America is going to have an industrial policy, let us at least define its central direction in a realistic manner. Let's concentrate on the big problem. Let us make growth the target.

Trying to direct the details of the American economy reminds me of Will Rogers' answer to the German U-boat menace. All you have to do, said Rogers, is to heat the ocean to the boiling point. That will take care of the U-boats. When someone asked Rogers how he intended to make the oceans boil, he replied, "Look, I have solved the big problem, you take care of the rest."

So, instead of trying to pick the winners, or simply increase or decrease government intervention for ideological reasons, let's try to rationalize interventions in the economy and give them a theme and a purpose—planning for growth by removing the obstacles to growth.

What we should be asking our government to do is not to plan everything for us or abandon everything to us—but to practice a kind of "climate control" to create the best possible conditions for real growth.

Let government fashion the climate of growth and opportunity while free market forces handle the microeconomic issues and seek out the winners.

If growth is going to be the objective, then government should take the lead in eliminating the bias against savings and investment in our tax system. It's difficult to encourage investment when we have double taxation on savings, when we create disincentives to save and, indeed, incentives to spend.

What are some of the other barriers to growth? The uneven distribution of the corporate income tax, for one. Many of the high-growth firms listed on the American Stock Exchange have effective tax rates more than double those of the Fortune 100 companies. That unfair tax burden stifles their growth.

As a matter of fact, the average corporate income tax paid by companies listed on our exchange amounts to 32.6 percent while the average corporate income tax paid by companies among the Fortune 100 is somewhat less than 17 percent. Older, larger industries have had special treatments built into their tax codes. The tax benefits that have been handed out tend to be for capital-intensive industries that aren't necessarily the winners. We should redress these equities that punish smaller, innovative companies that are, as you know, the greatest source of new jobs.

Government should also be providing more tax incentives for research and development by American industry. We don't need to channel or direct that research. The market is going to take care of that. But we do need incentives for our people to make the long-term investments and take those high risks that will bring profits and markets and leadership in the future.

Government must support vocational training and worker re-training, hopefully on a job, to help our work force match the skills required to keep this economy on the frontier of growth. Unless labor is convinced they will be full participants in America's growth, they can hardly be expected to support the progressive policies we believe are going to lead to that growth.

Government must step up its efforts at regulatory reform and insist that cost effectiveness be carefully considered. It's one thing to protect society from some of the unwanted consequences of mindless growth and it's another to starve it by strangling growth altogether.

Government can take the lead in demanding that our trading partners dismantle their barriers to American goods and cease their illegal unfair subsidies that cheat us out of markets—and growth—we have earned.

Perhaps most important, a government committed to real growth can help to dispel the distrust that has stood for so long between our public and private sectors. Government can be the catalyst that brings together our workers and our businessmen and women, our industrialists, and our academics—not to direct and control our economy, but to discuss these issues and strive for consensus on broad goals, much as the Social Security Commission did so successfully.

I would suggest that not one member of that commission agreed with every finding. But I would also suggest that it may prove to be a landmark in terms of groups of such terribly polarized points of view coming together on an issue of such critical national importance.

But it's this kind of industrial policy that makes sense for America—

a policy in which government provides the climate and incentives for growth while leaving the mechanics to the marketplace.

Let's not kid ourselves. Even the most balanced and restrained industrial policy can never be a substitute for sound monetary and fiscal policies that create an environment in which firms expand, create jobs, and improve America's international competitiveness. Monetary and fiscal policies that are too tight or too loose will lead to higher interest rates, discourage investment, and stunt growth no matter how brilliantly we evolve any industrial policy.

We must resist the impulse to raise taxes or to postpone scheduled tax cuts and we must reduce the budget deficit. It's difficult to envision robust economic growth in the context of $200 billion deficits throughout the 1980s and their inevitable pressure on interest rates.

No part of the federal budget can be immune from scrutiny. And the tale that the markets are telling us today will be a very different tale in the latter part of 1983 if no action has been taken on the reduction of these deficits.

In fiscal year 1985, fully 47 percent of the budget will go to the so-called entitlement programs such as Medicare and Social Security; 34 percent will go to defense; and 12 percent will be used to pay interest on the national debt. We simply cannot consecrate 93 percent of our spending and still hope to reduce the budget deficit.

Today, the long-awaited economic recovery is finally visible in the statistics and the indicators. We're feeling the lift of recovery and the energy and excitement and enthusiasm of emerging growth.

Yet America has paid a heavy, heavy price for the glowing embers of growth we see today in the ashes of recession. We have got to shield those embers with sound monetary and fiscal policies so the winds of economic change will fan them, not extinguish them. We need the kind of balanced approach to industrial policy that will allow those embers to ignite into the self-sustaining fire of growth.

If we succeed, and I have a funny feeling we're going to, there will no longer be any need to ask the question, "Why is growth important?" The answer will be self-evident and it will be right for America.

W. THOMAS J. GRIFFIN

What the Investor Looks For

I believe that my firm has indeed established something rather special in its approach to growth industries in that we combine an international perspective with an extremely strong team of investors, consultants, and analysts here in the United States.

G.T. is a truly international company, investing in all the major markets of the world, and for clients from about fifteen different countries. However, my mission today is to give you some indication of the role we play in the high technology part of our business. It starts, as all good businesses should, with the needs of our clients. For Europeans, as you can imagine, it is next to impossible to monitor the electronics stocks in Silicon Valley and elsewhere. They have difficulty in telling the difference between an Apple and an Amdahl or between a Tandem and a Tandon or even a Tandy. They are, therefore, in many cases happy to delegate the role of evaluating and investing in these stocks. About three and a half years ago, we established our first fund to serve these needs. It is called G.T. Technology Fund and it now concentrates on companies with between $150 million and $1 billion of annual sales. Last summer we started a second fund, called G.T. Applied Science Fund, and it invests in companies with sales up to $150 million and includes quite a number of private placements in smaller unlisted companies. The shareholders in both funds are mainly institutional, and in comparing notes with our clients, we find that even with the holdings in G.T. Technology Fund, there is curiously little duplication between our list and theirs.

Our team, which has its office in Menlo Park, is headed by my partner, George Shott, who has been working as an analyst of and investor in high technology industries for some twenty-five years. He has built up a band of analysts and consultants who work exclusively with us and give us access to many of the leading venture capitalists on the West Coast and to executives of most of the major companies there. Collectively, they bring an extraordinary depth and variety of knowledge to our group. The latest member of our team, for instance, is an eminent epidemiologist who spent a number of years as a senior member of the World Health Organization, and he is guiding us through the labyrinth of the new biotechnology industries.

Our main thrust, however, is concentrated primarily in investments that fall into the broad category of electronics, and within that industry it is concentrated in developing growth companies—that is, if you look at the familiar "S"-curve of growth, we are aiming at the second segment: after the formative stage, but before maturity. The electronics industry at present ranks ninth or tenth in size in the United States. Within ten years it will be number two.

Where do we stand in our approach to growth industries? It seems to us that the key and the main driving force is the need for productivity. This applies to all mature industries and to all mature economies. Many industries are either in decline or, at best, static, due to overexpansion in the 1960s and 1970s. All have a desperate need for greater productivity—some to compete and some just to stay alive. For many of these industries the threat of Japanese competition is the catalyst that has forced change on them. The Japanese, as we all know, are ruthlessly competitive with each other, as well as with all of us, and we ignore that fact at our peril.

At the same time as these pressures have been growing, modern technology has been providing some answers. Perhaps the most important contributor has been the microprocessor which for a number of years has been developing at a compound growth rate in computer power of 20 percent to 25 percent per annum. The cost to the user has been decreasing at a similar rate. These developments are pointing up the potential for whole new industries, some of which we already have with us but many of which have scarcely been conceived. We at G.T., therefore, are concentrating our investments in areas where the solving of productivity problems is of critical importance. This is taking us away from games and toys and even from micro-computers, where the number of manufacturers has become excessive and where the need for a shakeout is evident. Rather, we are looking to CAD/CAM and computer-aided engineering, to telecommunications and data communications, and to local area networks. Above all, we are looking to particular areas of software, especially those where individual companies have established themselves in providing a service to a specific industry which offers the potential for repeat business. HBO, a local company in Atlanta, and the hospital field in which it operates, would be a good case in point.

We also pay great attention to what we consider the key shortage in the development of these industries, namely, engineers. This shortage

will persist for at least the next ten years, even if the universities expand their output greatly. In fact, major companies in technology industries are already providing substantial support for professors of engineering to ensure a supply of graduate students.

The shortage of engineers will also have an effect on the location of
these industries (though less so in the case of software companies). It
will force the major companies to locate where the engineers want to
live. Almost certainly, when the history comes to be written, we will
find that the major development of these industries took place where
three critical conditions were provided. First, proximity to universities;
second, proximity to a major airport; and third, a good quality of life.
The well-known relationship between Stanford University and Hewlett-
Packard, and the founding of the Stanford Science Park and the whole
subsequent development of Silicon Valley is a story that is being imi-
tated in a number of places. The electronic companies that set up in
Buffalo or Detroit are going to have a tough time competing for graduate engineers.

The other key factor, of course, is management. This may seem
blindingly obvious but it is surprising how many investors get beguiled
by the idea of the next 256K widget and how many companies are formed
by bright engineers who have nothing but bright engineering thoughts
to guide them. This is a classic British mistake which I fear gets re-
peated all too often even this side of the Atlantic. Most of my colleagues' work is, in fact, devoted to trying to identify managements with
a full range of talents in marketing and finance, as well as in engineering, necessary to build a company—in fact, the abilities to build a major company in a big market. Thus, we avoid companies that are run
by promoters and we avoid "Me Too" companies—that is, those that
claim to do IBM's business a bit cheaper. We stick, instead, to companies that are bringing something new to the table and that can develop a significant niche in the market. To do this we concentrate on
keeping up the best possible network of friends and allies in the industry, including both directors of major corporations and, at the other end
of the scale, many of the leading venture capitalists. The problem, of
course, is becoming ever more complex. There was a point at which
from Menlo Park, where we are located, you could find out almost
everything that was going on, but with the proliferation of new companies and with developments here in Atlanta and in North Carolina,
Texas, Colorado, and many other places, the game is becoming harder.
Nevertheless, we feel that the opportunities are so enormous that by
concentrating on the principles I have stated we can continue to flourish. If an IBM can renew itself and create whole new industries, there
is plenty of scope for the investor.

Of course, our investment in high technology industries is not confined to America. In Japan particularly, we have a major concentration in stocks that are benefiting from the new industrial revolution. Japanese competition in any element of the electronics industry that has a commodity aspect is extremely fierce. Where the Japanese skills at mass production can be wedded to the new technologies, Japan is in many instances unbeatable. From the point of view of the investor in Japan, however, this raises as many problems as it solves. Almost all of the Japanese electronics industry in which one can invest is contained in very large companies and, in most cases, the beneficial effects to the shareholder are diluted by the fact that these large companies are engaged in all sorts of other activities. A good instance would be Hitachi, which is a major producer of semiconductors and a significant factor in the computer industry, but 75 percent of their business is still in cyclical and slower growth products.

There are moves afoot to create an over-the-counter market and to encourage venture capital development. Indeed, Nomura alone is reputed to have some seventy companies under its wing which might be listed on an over-the-counter market and many of these would be in the electronics and bio-technology industries. Nevertheless, the present effect of the structure of the Japanese market is to limit the possibilities for investment in exceptionally rapidly growing companies.

In Europe the picture is somewhat different. France used to be a particularly promising place to invest, with a number of very rapidly growing companies, especially in the defense industry. All that was changed by the victory of Monsieur Mitterand in the summer of 1981, and both politically and as regards the currency, the odds are stacked against the investor.

The U.K. now presents the most promising scene. A number of major companies have shown very rapid growth in recent years, averaging 30 percent or more compounded, but more exciting for the future is the burgeoning of an over-the-counter market and the development of numerous small companies. The rate of registration of new companies is at an all-time high by a considerable margin and both along the road westward from London to Bristol, and in Scotland, between Glasgow and Edinburgh, there is a tremendous growth of high technology companies. The British have always been extremely good at inventing things and we hope that under the beneficent rule of Mrs. Thatcher they will become better at making money out of them.

One curious phenomenon may be worth noting: The British have bought more computers per head of the population than any other nation. What the hell they are all doing with them is anybody's guess but maybe things are stirring. It is also interesting to note that the same association between growth industries and universities is occurring in the U.K. and we are rapidly reaching the stage when every self-respecting university will have its associated science park.

Earlier on I mentioned our interest in bio-technology. I must admit that this is still in its embryo stage, although I think we are making significant progress. For myself, however, I am still having problems telling the difference between a monoclonal antibody and a genetic engineer. The industry is, of course, still at an early stage of development, possibly akin to the state of the electronics industry in the 1960s. It is at the stage where scientific knowledge is advancing very rapidly but the practical applications that create major businesses are only now beginning to emerge. However, we have identified in this country some forty companies at varying stages of development of which about ten seem worthy of serious consideration as investments. We are also investing in a number of European companies such as Novo in Denmark and Astra and Fortia in Sweden which are among the leaders in their respective fields. There is, of course, also a great deal of work going on in the U.K. but, as so often happens, the brilliant scientific work has not been carried through so effectively into business applications. In Japan, the significant advances and the major opportunities are embedded in large companies, many of which we have held for some years.

In this brief survey I have left out many service industries which themselves offer possibilities for rapid growth in order to concentrate on the main thrust of our investment policy. Please accept that this is due to pressure of time rather than lack of interest.

In closing, I want to point again to the two very powerful forces we see at work. The first is the desperate need for productivity, which is driving both companies and governments into hard decisions. And the second is the shortage of engineers, which will force decisions of a different kind.

We recognize that there will be times when high technology stocks are grossly overvalued, but we believe that by concentrating on these industries we are offering our clients the possibility of backing exceptional managements in sectors of the market which will show the greatest value added.

STEPHEN A. LIEBER

In the world of economic growth opportunities, the horizons often seem so unlimited that we tend to overlook fundamental problems. The fundamental problems with growth and growth opportunity stem from an organic social structure that has a life cycle. As investors, we are all faced with a recognition that, when we start looking for growth opportunities, we are trying to deal with the immature which can become mature, which can become obsolescent, and which can die.

Thus, we are engaged in a risk-related strategy, which we must subject to analysis in order to see clearly when risks outweigh prospective rewards. In reflecting upon this problem in our organization over many years, we think about it not only abstractly but in terms of companies, when at a research meeting we say, "Where is it going, is it on the rise or is it on the fall?" Is this business going in a direction that is so strong that even an obsolescent management will prove successful and, if so, why and how?

We recognize that as companies grow in experience and in size, to get to Professor Olson's earlier observations, they are like cities, states, countries. There is an encrustation. There is a risk factor. And we have basically taken the point of view that the opportunity for consistent growth performance is greatest in the simplest, freshest areas where complexity of activities and of management structure does not obscure major trends.

I would say that we break down our view of investment opportunity into five basic areas: First, the easy, straightforward growth. I refer to a management that is producing a simply described product or service and doing it well, dealing in either a rapidly growing market or one in which their special skills permit a high level of penetration of a market that is not fully exploited by a competing product or service. Very direct, very simple; more often than not, companies like this either arrive at a terminal phase fairly early or they go on to a second stage of growth.

The second stage is one in which they have enlarged their sphere—either economically by adding on a product or service or geographically, or both. Further, they must be able to expand without a deterioration in the quality of their service or production. There is no better example than the fast food industry. Look at McDonald's. Look at the great supermarkets. Look what Winn-Dixie has done over generations, basically holding to a narrow line.

The third basic area is that of companies that broaden their field of endeavor. They see new related products and they go after them. They're stretching. The risk increases. There is still the geometry from the small capital base. They may make it.

The fourth is where they innovatively broaden the field they serve. This is where a company—such as Hewlett-Packard—can perceive of the opportunity in not just a product, but a product concept. They enlarge the industry's product or service base. They provide a leadership factor in a variety of activities, enhancing the overall economic opportunity. That's harder and fewer succeed, but we look at them.

In the fifth basic growth area are the companies that recognize that they have achieved diversity, breadth, and leadership and are faced with obsolescence: obsolescence in their product lines, possibly obsolescence in their approach.

They recognize and effectively face obsolescence. Then they do something about it to sustain their growth. We see constant attempts by major leadership companies in this country to achieve such a reinvigoration. Look at what has been going on recently at Sears, Roebuck in that effort to revitalize a great, broad, and in many ways immobile, entity.

Our goals, then, are to recognize the risk factors, not to be limited to any one area of expertise (whether it be technology or transportation or services) but to go out and find the recognizable growth opportunities. Let me mention one measure of success that we've used in our first phase (that is, the relatively simple businesses) and in the second group (those that have enlarged their spheres). It is when the company in which we have invested is offered the opportunity to be bought out by a larger, more diverse company that has decided to gain entry to a market by acquiring rather than by building.

For example, General Electric decided a couple of years ago that it should have been in the CAD/CAM business and it went in and bought a CAD/CAM company. That acquired company doubtless will have satisfied its management and shareholders very much by being taken over by General Electric. The original concept has been satisfactorily exploited and it has achieved growth. Hopefully, it has now become the catalyst for growth for a larger company. Our experience in The Evergreen Fund, incidentally, is that over the last ten and a half years ninety-nine companies that were in our portfolio have been so taken over.

Now the fundamental ingredient that we really look for, being diverse in our approach, is obviously management skill. The vitality of management is fundamental, whether it is one man or a crew. More often it is one man who either can sustain the whole organization or can create a group that sustains an organization.

It seems that you need a great ability to keep the adrenals going to run growth companies. The more I see it, the more I think of it as an athletic kind of competitive, unrelenting, well-trained, dedicated mind able to sustain excitement.

Plenty of people can do all of that naturally with no judgment and no experience, and then they have to find the judgment and the experience. This is the totally challenging aspect of looking for investments and, in my experience, it's been quite wonderful to find it in so many diverse fields. I would like to share some of our approaches to looking for fields where we might see some of the adrenal vitality and straightforward opportunity within the lines I've cited.

Again, we are not committed to any single area. We try to think through what's happening in the economy, and we think that people's adrenals and people's abilities are stimulated by change. They are stimulated not only by the change of their own invention of products, not only by the change of the technologies through which they visualize their only self-satisfaction, but by changes in the society which they are quick enough to perceive.

One of the really impressive areas of capital appreciation opportunity for us over recent years has been in banks. The banking industry is undergoing substantial change. In effect, it is experiencing deregulation. I believe it's headed toward the end of the restrictions on interstate banking.

You've seen more such activity in the Southeast than anyplace else, where you can find a grandfather clause bringing North Carolina National Bank down into Florida as a major presence, seeking a growth market. This was a management whose adrenals were functioning very well indeed and creating opportunity for shareholders on a couple of levels: at the level of the parent company, with a creative management, and at the level of the smaller bank that was the attractive vehicle for NCNB to take over.

We've also found great opportunities in smaller, regional newspapers. We looked at the technology over the last several years and we saw that an industry that basically was functioning within a nineteenth-century adaptation of a fifteenth-century framework in typesetting and in printing had benefited by this vast shift to computer typeset and offset. We raised the question of who would make the most of this opportunity in a changing situation.

Was it going to be the producers of the capital goods, the possessors of the innovative technology, or was it going to be the newspaper managements that would be able to look at the pressroom and say, "We don't need all of that stuff"? It was obvious. I think the profit margin of the smaller newspaper in this country has been greatly enhanced. The chains have become much more profitable enterprises. Organizations like Lee Enterprises, like Harte Hanks, were able to take the larger earnings and use them in a creative growth framework by saying, "Now we'll get the little fellows in another town or another city or another good small metropolitan area by buying out their operation. We will put in the technology, and we will improve the profit margin so we leverage out."

This kind of approach to change is attractive to us. Currently we are looking at the whole area of software networking, not merely in terms of the opportunity for the firms who will be producing software, but also for the people who control the data bases.

Look at the publishers who for decades have been assembling and accumulating information. The technology has now arrived at a stage where it can be handled much more rationally, and I think you'll see interesting moves, such as Warner Communications going after Harcourt Brace. There are many interesting growth implications in this area. People are going to exploit their data bases intensively, including the Dun and Bradstreets of this world, Commerce Clearing House, and Prentice-Hall. Each has an exploitable treasure trove of data for the electronics age. They haven't fully realized it. Theirs will be a recurring utilized resource just as were the great movie libraries, as cable TV came in, and as network television needed products. Even Coca-Cola Company is in the movie production business.

In summary, let me say that we focus on change, recognize the dynamics, look to the reality of that life cycle of corporations, and seek to benefit by being in the right stages—hopefully at the right time.

EDWARD J. MATHIAS

Let me give you just a little background information pertaining to the New Horizons Fund. To my knowledge, we are the largest investor in the country in what is known as emerging growth stocks. New Horizons is a no-load mutual fund founded in 1960. Today we have assets that exceed $1.3 billion. The fund owns over 160 publicly traded securities and has over 71,000 shareholders.

What I want to do before describing our investment approach and the criteria we use is to look at the environment in which we as investors operate. All of us have a preoccupation with day-to-day events and a tendency to miss major structural changes.

It's worthy of note that successful investors often prosper by identifying major trends and investing accordingly. Today, we don't want to fail to recognize that this is a period of dramatic change and that there are some powerful forces at work that show no signs of reversing. There are numerous dislocations, but the flip side of the coin is that from the dislocations come opportunities.

The preoccupation in our country today seems to be greatly skewed toward the negative, although it's not as pronounced as it was several years ago. We all know the litany: We are a mature nation, in economic stagnation; we are noncompetitive worldwide; we must look to the Japanese as the prototype; and we have insurmountable structural problems. I could go on and on.

Yet, when you delve beneath the surface, a different picture emerges. There are strong signs of life throughout the economy. What you conclude is that we are going through a transition period. What we're seeing is, in many respects, a two-tiered economy.

There are problems with the basic industries and, in many respects, they are noncompetitive. On the other hand, the U.S. has a tremendous number of new industries developing, and they tend to fall in two general categories. One is technology driven. The other is somewhat similar, but we view it differently. It is a shifting of the infrastructure toward service and information processing—what Peter Drucker has called the "knowledge industries."

To us, these changes are very deep-seated. Many were fostered by the need to solve the problems of the 1970s. Productivity comes most readily to mind. Others result from worldwide competitive forces. Tax incentives legislated in the late 1970s have given a tremendous impetus to innovation and growth. Not only changes in the capital gains tax and that on unearned income, but also changes to ERISA (the Employees Retirement Income Security Act) have unleashed huge amounts of pension money to fuel the future growth of the U.S. economy.

We also are experiencing some changes in demographics. It's hard to believe that with a 10-percent unemployment rate we may have a shortage in the labor force in the late 1980s, but such a development seems highly likely. Also, in the 1970s there were a tremendous number of technological innovations. What we are going to see in the 1980s is companies and industries developing to apply these technologies.

Let me look at some specifics now in terms of the investment climate. There are three points that I want to make. The first is that the entrepreneurial spirit is alive and well. Anyone who has visited San Francisco or Silicon Valley in California would certainly attest to that. Second, we have planted the seeds for future growth. Third, from an investor's standpoint, the universe of attractive new growth companies is expanding almost exponentially.

Let me first discuss venture capital. In the early 1970s, virtually no money went into venture capital. In 1979, we had $170 million. In 1982, we had $1.4 billion. Most of the money last year went into business start-ups. The investment returns in venture capital have been extremely high. This has attracted more money and has encouraged a lot of entrepreneurs to go out and start businesses.

One thing we can say is that the $1.4 billion in 1982 will require probably four to five times that amount before the companies come public. Thus, there will be a tremendous need for capital to finance growth in this area over the next few years.

Historically, venture capital has been concentrated in New England and on the West Coast around San Francisco. One thing that is happening today is a tremendous dispersion, and the Southeast will be a primary beneficiary.

A lot of attention has been devoted to such business-location issues as the quality of life, where engineers want to live, and the best business climate. The Southeast qualifies in all respects and I expect that, over the next few years, you'll see a tremendous amount of venture capital activity in the region.

Let me look now at new issues in the public market. It's very important that entrepreneurs and venture capitalists have access to the public markets. The stock market encountered problems in the 1970s and this dampened interest in new issues. As a result, only thirty companies came public in 1974–1975, raising $316 million. In the last three years, more than 900 companies have come public with an initial market value of over $6 billion. In 1983, the trend continues. What I think we can see is that the stock market, acting as an allocator of capital, recognizes the structural changes that are taking place.

Let me turn now to the over-the-counter market. This is a very vibrant force in our economy. It's really the spawning ground for tomorrow's growth companies. Look at what has happened. You had 2,500 companies in 1977 and 3,300 in 1982. The number of shares traded has gone up to a tremendous extent. This can be explained partially by the fact that today there seem to be more traders than investors.

Also, we've seen institutions beginning to come into the over-the-counter market. Historically, this market has been the purview of the individual investor. But now we see major institutions, primarily pension funds, increasingly active. So what we have is a great deal of interest in small growth companies and also increasingly large amounts of capital that are available.

Let me now turn to the New Horizons Fund and how we go about identifying and evaluating emerging growth companies. We have sailed under the same flag since 1960 and what we're trying to do is crystal clear. We want to invest in small, rapidly growing companies. There are two dimensions to it from our standpoint: the first being "growth" and the second being "small." We're talking about "small" relative to the standards of the public market, not relative to your small local business.

Our target is to find companies that can grow at 20 percent a year compound. An investor should never ignore the powerful concept of compounding. At an annual growth rate of 5 percent, a dollar becomes $1.28 in five years. If you grow at 70 percent, it becomes $14.20.

We see a lot of companies that can grow at very high rates, and you can see how the mathematics work. What we're trying to do is to pick out companies that can grow at high rates, providing a substantial premium over the nominal rate of GNP. Our expectation is that, over time, this compounding will work for the shareholder and that the company's increased value will be recognized in the stock market.

The second dimension is size. To us, the best measure of a company's size is pretax income. There are other measures, of course. Capitalization is one, but that changes dramatically as the market goes up and down. You can look at after-tax income, but then you run into tax havens, research and development partnerships, various tax credits, and so on.

You can look at sales, but the sales of a grocery chain are very different in terms of their margins than what you might find in a technology company. We have found that pretax income is the best measure for us. The median in our portfolio is $12.8 million, to give some idea of the size.

Ours is a company orientation. We call it the life cycle concept. Some have called it the aging process; others call it the S curve.

What we're trying to do is to be early in terms of a company's corporate development. We want to be there when it's going through the rapid stages of growth. An example of a local company where we are a very major shareholder would be Management Science America Inc. We identified the company soon after it went public and we have stayed with it. It's grown at a very high rate in terms of earnings and the stock has appreciated handsomely.

The second element important to us is to be early in terms of investor awareness or recognition. That has become more and more difficult as additional investors have turned their attention to this sector of the market.

When there were relatively few institutions focusing on the over-the-counter market, investors had much more time than is available today. Now good investment ideas have a relatively short life cycle before others recognize them.

Conceptually what we are doing is very simple. It's a proven approach that has worked over a long period of time. The real key is execution. Let me highlight the primary elements of New Horizons' approach.

The first is an emphasis on fundamental research. We think of this as doing our homework. We have ten analysts who work full time for the fund and are recognized experts in small companies.

Second, we operate in an area where there is considerable value added. There is just less competition in analyzing a small company than there would be in analyzing an IBM, a Burroughs, or an NCR; not that you can't find advantages in those larger companies, but the competition is certainly more intense.

The academicians have said the small-company area is "inefficient." They call it the "small company effect" and claim that, historically, investors have always earned higher returns in small companies.

Our investment horizon is two to three years. You have to tailor it to the company. With some companies, you can look only at a year ahead. The personal computer area would be an example. Clearly at some point there will be a shakeout. With others, say a sound retailing concept, you might be able to look ahead five to seven years.

Almost by definition, we're going to end up with representation in the fastest growing segments of the economy. There is no shortage of opportunities today. There's been a lot of fanfare about genetic engineering. As yet, the company has made few profits, but the potential is awesome. Our strategy in an area like this is to wait until you can see the earnings.

Pharmaceutical delivery systems represent another form of technology, with Key Pharmaceutical in Miami being an example. They market a patch that you can put on your body to release chemicals on a time basis.

Robotics and intelligent machines are other technologies. Automatics, a company that just came public, is really the first public robotics company. There are a number of others on the drawing board. This technology ties into the need for improved productivity.

The need to tie computers together in networks provides another opportunity. You are all familiar with the so-called office of the future. There are also tremendous changes taking place in semiconductor technology. We are going to what they call VLSI—very large-scale integrated circuits. A practical description of VLSI is incorporating more functions on a single chip. There is also a lot going on in the whole area of consumer electronics. Software, which offers tremendous opportunities, is an area that typically has not required a great deal of capital.

All innovation does not necessarily come from technology firms. Warehouse retailing, for instance, is a new concept. It's starting on the West Coast with a firm called the Price Company. A lot of changes are also taking place in distribution. One area that we find interesting is how you can bring technologies and services to small businesses.

Whether it be business forms or telecommunications equipment, there is a huge market out there for those who can figure out how to serve it efficiently.

I might mention the sources for our ideas. We maintain a network of contacts, and there's nothing more important in this business. We get ideas from shareholders and companies from which we currently have investments. We also have found regional brokerage firms to be a tremendous source of ideas because they tend to know the local companies. We have a longstanding relationship with brokerage firms such as Robinson-Humphrey in Atlanta. We use First Interstate, which is also in the Southeast, and there are a number of others.

Computer data bases have provided a dramatic breakthrough in our business because today you can identify and assess almost every public company from data readily available on the computer.

In summary, there is a tremendous amount of information available. We frequently observe that people always want to find the obscure company before anyone else. If you're going to be investing in growth companies, I would say don't dismiss the obvious. There is an old saying in the business, "Take the easy wins." Often you can just identify a company that for one reason or another you think has substantial growth potential. That is not a bad investment approach.

There's nothing magic about our analytical process. I think our edge comes in doing our homework. We have a phrase that the criteria or the principles that we apply stay relatively constant, but the companies and industries that meet them change.

A primary focus is on management. That is a key ingredient in successful companies. The one hard and fast rule we have is, given that we take a two-to-three-year horizon at a minimum, we make no investment without having met the management. The smaller the company, the more important the management. The executives own a majority of the shares and tend to be entrepreneurial in spirit. You'd like to have some idea as to their thinking and what they're likely to do.

I mentioned the 20-percent annual growth potential we look for in companies. A change now over what took place in the 1970s is that the unit growth has become more important than price growth. If you look at the oil companies, considered the growth area of the late 1970s, they weren't pumping more oil. In effect, they were growing by raising their price.

We would much prefer to have a company that is shipping more units out the door. The best example of that is the semiconductor business where they have tremendous growth in unit volume. We also look for firms with financial strength and high levels of profitability, but which also are reinvesting in the company.

Most of the companies in which we invest pay nominal dividends, if any. The money is being plowed back for the shareholders. That has particular advantages for taxable investors in that it's something like a savings account.

You always look for a distinctive competence, something that gives the company a competitive edge and will allow it to prosper and grow. We have always liked companies that have some control over their own destiny. We used to say we would avoid any company subject to government regulation or interference. That is now an impossibility, but we do tend to avoid highly regulated industries.

We consider several other factors to be important in small-company investing. The first is diversification. This is an inherently aggressive style and some mistakes are inevitable. If you don't make them, you're probably not taking enough risks. Unfortunately, we have made our share. But we have also learned by experience that, if you're investing in companies early in their life cycle, you cannot identify the next Digital Equipment with any assurance. You just have to diversify and recognize that serendipity is important in this kind of investing. Our concept is to seed a portfolio with what we call ideas that have breakaway potential.

You also have to recognize there is a difference between a stock and a company. With any investment the price is important. There are two factors: One is what do you get and the second is what do you pay for it. You live in peril if you forget that. Our idea is that you cannot fine-tune valuations in this sector of the market, so we watch for extremes. We are trying to identify the anomalies, not the arbitrage between stock that is selling at twelve times earnings and one that is selling at thirteen times earnings.

I want to emphasize that this is a very volatile sector of the market. It amplifies market movement both ways. While it is contrary to human nature, to be successful in this type of investing, you must neither panic at market bottoms nor become overenthusiastic when times are good. Investors have to keep a check on their emotions.

In today's environment, we see tremendous growth opportunities. You have to admit, though, that these have not gone unrecognized in the stock market. This has been a period of extraordinary performance for small companies.

Just as an example, the New Horizons Fund is up 192.1 percent over five years. The market is up 93.6 percent. Since August 13, 1982, when the market turned, we're up 79.3 and Standard and Poors is up 49.9. That type of relative edge, to my thinking, just cannot be sustained indefinitely.

In looking at growth companies today, you have to be conscious that a lot of them have high relative valuations and also that this is a popular area. It's an area of tremendous interest and if you have anything of a contrarian bent, you certainly would not be in the small-technology stocks today. On the other hand, we believe we are relatively early in what could be a sustained economic cycle and a secular bull market.

Moreover, the sky is not cloudless. It is a very hot new-issue market. History suggests that it will end more with a bang than with a whimper, though we certainly hope that is not the case. Greed certainly has overtaken fear in the small-company area. Expectations are very high. That is clear from the fact that price-earnings ratios have increased dramatically.

Finally, today's glamour area is no longer energy. It's technology, and things are changing in the technology area. There is much more competition. It's hard to believe that some of the companies that are starting up in venture capital are not going to bump into each other. These are not all going to turn up to be $500 million companies within the next three or four years. I feel fairly confident of that; the question is which ones will survive and prosper.

Interestingly, when you talk to people starting companies, they don't have that overview. They all see themselves as unique, with no competition. Yet these technologies are going to dovetail much sooner than has been the case in the last few years. What we can say is that in the technology area, life cycles probably are going to get shorter and shorter. There's going to be a continual leapfrogging of companies. It's going to be a very risky area in which to invest and investors are going to have to look for the new technologies and the companies with distinctive products.

Investing in small growth companies, then, is a proven concept. But it is not designed to be a total program. This is not an area where investors should have all their money. It's not a get-rich-quick approach. Yet there are tremendous opportunities today for the knowledgeable buyer. With patience—and that is the one word I would underline—investing in a portfolio of emerging growth companies will prove highly rewarding, and the rewards will take the form of superior investment returns.

DISCUSSION

WINER: I'm Leon Winer. Several people have mentioned the coming shake-out in microcomputers. I would be interested in knowing who the survivors will be. Which will be the successful companies?

GRIFFIN: Well, there's a little company called IBM that I think might survive. I guess that Apple is really going to survive, so that would be another choice. Obviously Digital Equipment Corporation is going to be there for as long and as far as the eye can see. But I think some of the smaller ones that can't get shelf space are going to have problems. There are now, I believe, 150 firms in this area, and I can't see how all of them are going to survive.

The other point I would like to make is that the Japanese competition in this area has really not impacted here at all, because they are still so busy selling into their own market. The two major producers in Japan, NEC and Sharp, now have, I think, 75 percent of their own market.

Now their market is about one third the size of the U.S. market in terms of microcomputers, so that makes those two companies extremely powerful. If they do move in, they could well have an impact, too.

FEINBERG: I'm Bob Feinberg of the House Banking Committee. Given all of this ferment, the question that I'd like to ask both of the growth portfolio managers is: Are there opportunities in playing the opposite side? What I'm looking at are the large companies that are not going to be the IBM survivors. They are also not small enough to grow, their products are mature, and in this environment they can expect to be left behind. Given the growth in the technology industry and the fact that there will be some bumps, should one look for stocks to play on the short side at times when the market seems to be ready for that, maybe during big corrections or in the next bear market, even if that's two or three years away?

MATHIAS: At some point that would be advisable strategy but the timing is the key question. That depends on the investor's own psychology and ability to predict the market. It does look like, in this environment, a lot of the smaller technology companies are more highly valued than the larger and that gap should close. I think there are some opportunities in the larger technology companies that have characteristics that equate with success: good products, good management, strong market share, and so on.

KOCH: Look at an amazing company like Apple. It's a company just a few years old that comes up with some $84 to $85 million in earnings and $600 million in sales, and they double employees every year. Last year they had 3,000 employees and this year they have 6,000. That's phenomenal but it's market driven.

MATHIAS: Many of you who manage companies know the internal pressures that high growth brings. Absorbing large numbers of new people creates problems and this is especially true in northern California, where the competition for people is intense. We monitor this and consider hyper growth a cautionary flag. You just can't absorb too rapid a rate of change for large periods.

WINSTON: James Winston. Congress has just passed a massive transportation tax. Do any of the panelists see any companies that may benefit from this in the long run?

LIEBER: You are talking, I presume, about the possibilities that capital gas companies will participate in utilizing the so-called road funds. Well, I think you saw a classical rapid response to that in the stock market. Whether it was buying Barber Greene for asphalt road-making machinery, cement stocks, or Caterpillar. The tax funds certainly will have an impact on these depressed capital goods and raw material supplying fields; whether it will have as significant an impact as the emergence from the recession itself, I don't know. I should regard it as a favorable, though not conclusive, factor in the direction of lifting up the demand base for these industries.

INTRODUCTION OF SPEAKER

John H. Weitnauer, Jr.

Robert H. Waterman, Jr., is recognized as one of the nation's leading experts in business management. Among other contributions, he has given all of us a fresh way of looking at successful companies and at the elements that make them tick. And he has reminded us that the best managed American firms don't have to take a back seat to anyone—a timely reminder that we can all take to heart.

As a director of McKinsey & Company, Waterman is responsible for a major research project in organization design and development, one of the most significant and ambitious undertakings in McKinsey's history. Most of us know him, however, because of a best-selling book that he co-authored as an outgrowth of his research into U.S. management.

In reviewing the managements of 43 of America's leading corporations, Waterman detected a common thread that seemed to be shared by the high-performance firms. He found that certain common elements distilled from his research were present in consistently profitable and innovative firms, no matter what their specialized fields happened to be. Thus he found a commonality between successful firms as diverse as IBM Corporation, Procter & Gamble, 3M Company, and Delta Air Lines.

So intrigued was he by the repetition of these characteristics that he teamed with Thomas J. Peters to write a book detailing their findings. Specifically, the book emphasized several characteristics that emerged over and over in their research—such factors as an emphasis on people and a willingness to take risks.

The book, which was published late in 1982 and moved quickly onto the national bestseller list, is In Search of Excellence: Lessons from America's Best-Run Companies. *We expect him to share some of those lessons.*

The New York Times *describes* In Search of Excellence *as a book that "points the way to the future for our entire economy"—a book that looks to American models, not to Japan, for a blueprint to business success. If it is true that our nation needs a success story more than ever, Waterman and his colleague have provided it in this study.*

Waterman joined McKinsey's San Francisco office in 1961. His projects at McKinsey have included research into a broad range of organization and strategy problems in a wide variety of industries, including banking, high technology, mining, and forest products.

ROBERT H. WATERMAN, JR.

Management Excellence and Growth

Let me outline some of the highlights of our research and some of its practical aspects. At press interviews and on radio talk shows, people ask, "What is the one incident that has been most striking in all your research?" Well, the research started about five years ago, so it is hard to imagine what that one thing might be. But in the early part of the book there's a diagram showing one of our clients' new-product introduction processes. It is a big circle that shows all the different departments involved. They are interconnected by, if you count them, 223 different lines. These lines represent different committees that are supposed to meet with each other or different formal approval processes that are supposed to take place before a new product is actually introduced by this company.

This company was asking us why they couldn't introduce more new products. This diagram was drawn by one of our client's people, who said, "You know, here's the reason." He showed it to us and he's absolutely right; it is the reason.

The surprising thing is that when I tell audiences about this or show it on a screen, people identify with it. They say, "Yeah, that's our new-product introduction process." Or "that's our capital budgeting process," or "that's our loan approval process." You name your process in large companies and you find that same sort of thing. The real irony is that if you take every one of those lines one by one and look at them, they are all rational. They are all done by perfectly well-meaning people who are trying to solve some current problems; but if you put it all together, it doesn't work. It doesn't work and so you get what Andrew Pettigrew, one of our favorite organizational researchers, calls the inertial properties of large organizations. We were worried about big organizations since that's our client base. Pettigrew asked why big organizations have so much trouble moving and adjusting despite the fact that individuals inside understand that the environment is changing and they probably should change, too. Why does this inertia exist? Well, if you look at that diagram, it starts to become obvious.

One study we looked at from the National Science Foundation shows that small companies were out-innovating the large companies per R & D dollar spent by a factor of 24. And the medium-sized companies were out-innovating the large companies by a factor of 4. Also consider Burton Klein's research in *Dynamic Economics,* where he looked at fifty major innovations over the last half century. In no case that he studied was the major innovation brought forward by the industry leader at the time.

What got us started were questions like these about corporate innovation. Our research was triggered by an event held on July 4, 1979, when the managing board of Royal Dutch/Shell Group asked Tom Peters and me to speak on innovation. These thoughts were floating around in our minds and we used the occasion as a sort of rallying point to consolidate some of the information.

We went out and talked to Hewlett-Packard and to 3M and we talked to some of the other large companies that we considered innovative. The question was, Is it always true that big companies aren't innovative? So we picked some that we thought were innovative, like IBM and 3M, and started reading about them and talking to them.

At that time our thoughts were very ill formed. The Royal Dutch/Shell board wasn't that enthusiastic; they said, "Well, it's interesting but it doesn't really apply to us." They were probably right about that. But then we owed some feedback sessions to these companies we had talked to and so we got back to them. They were really excited about it and they encouraged us. That's what got the whole project going, and then we secured some funding.

What we did was select about 100 big companies that are thought of as being well-managed and thought to be innovative in some sense. So our original criterion was whether people thought of these companies as innovative. Then we applied some pretty rigorous financial screens over a twenty-year period, using six different measures. They must have demonstrated a certain rate of growth and return on investment. They had to have outperformed their industry in four out of the six categories of long-term superiority. It wasn't good enough to be just well thought of and thought of as innovative, they must have performed well too.

So that narrowed it down to the 43 companies that we talk about in the book. And we went from 100 down to the 43 based on the financial screens we used and by deleting European companies from the list because they did not represent a fair cross section of European business. We didn't talk about European companies in the book, although the findings are directionally the same.

Our research continues. We are still looking at companies. Our

Washington office recently completed a similar study for the American Business Conference. One of the most interesting things they found is that, contrary to what a lot of people think, there are really top performing, high-growth companies in almost every industry. It doesn't have to be an explosive market; it doesn't have to be high tech, although obviously growth helps. They found it everywhere they looked, with companies creating their own niches.

So what we found after doing our research, and what I want to stress, are some of the characteristics of these excellent companies. I'll stress some of these main characteristics and give some examples, a few of which are in our book, and a few that aren't. I'll also try to highlight what I think are the most important points from a management standpoint or from the perspective of potential investors or observers of the economy.

An overriding theme that is difficult to grasp, but which probably is the most important, is found in the last chapter. We call it "loose-tight properties." People were asking us whether these companies were centralized or decentralized. The fact is they are some funny combination of both. They are very tight around the things they stand for and that they hold to be really important—the shared values. They are very tightly controlled around those dimensions. They are very decentralized around everything else.

Some people liken it to being good parents. If you are too tight with your children all the time, that doesn't work; if you are loose in every dimension, that doesn't work either. So it's a case of figuring out the right dimensions. And this is the artfulness of it, for I don't know any easy answer to figuring out the right dimensions around which to be tight and the right dimensions around which to be loose.

That's kind of an overriding theme that you will see throughout the book because the book really is, among other things, a study in ambiguity. We've discussed the importance of action but it is not as if these companies are without plans. It is just that they don't overdo it one way or the other.

So the contrast, the paradox between tight and loose dimensions, is an underlying theme that is implicit. We didn't bring it out very much because it's one of the harder things to understand. But unless you understand our biases on that, the book is apt to be overinterpreted. These companies don't all run around in free form all the time, but neither are they planning all the time.

I'll lump together some of the main characteristics under the heading "autonomy, action, entrepreneurship." Think about that 223-committee diagram I talked about earlier. One of the most surprising things to us as we first interviewed some of these companies was the small units. Our first interviews were with Hewlett-Packard, a $5 billion corporation that is broken up into approximately fifty divisions. We couldn't get our minds around that. Here we are, the consultants, the rationalists in the crowd, saying, "Gee, why is that? You ought to be able to consolidate some of those fifty divisions and save a lot of money." Obviously, they had too many facilities, too many chip-production facilities, too many R & D labs, too many engineers, too many salesmen, too many of this, too many of that. They explained patiently that, for them, what we call "suboptimal organization" is optimal. They are making a tradeoff between what I call a certain sloppiness around the organizational edges in order to get entrepreneurship and innovation.

We find the same characteristics as we look at more and more companies. I talked to J & J and they talk about getting big by staying small. Chairman Lew Lehr just reorganized 3M in 1981 and what did he do? He made the divisions smaller—took 90,000 employees and made the divisions smaller. Look at the Dana Corporation with its phenomenal productivity record. Look at Rene McPherson and now Gerald Mitchell, at Dana, who are very proud of their ninety store managers operating what are really little plants scattered around the field. Fletcher Byrom at Koppers, in a recent reorganization, divided something like five divisions into thirty. So the smallness factor is intriguing; it is an action device, an entrepreneurial device.

The idea is to be big but stay small some way or the other. It requires some obvious tradeoffs. You lose "efficiency" in that process. But what you gain are action and entrepreneurship. There's a people productivity element to it, too, because it's easier for the individual to identify with the smaller unit. This is the way Hewlett-Packard CEO John Young first explained his fifty units to us. He said, "Well, that's so the division manager knows everybody's name." He said that only partly tongue in cheek. You see, you identify with a 1,200-person division; it's much harder to identify with a unit a lot bigger. Emerson Electric plants employ around 600, for instance, competing effectively on a cost basis with General Electric.

We also found lots and lots of internal competition in the best sense of the term. We picked that up at Procter & Gamble, which has been doing it for a long time. Competition among brand managers at Procter & Gamble has been alive and well ever since Chairman Neil McElroy joined the firm way back when. We found competition among divisions and performance "shootouts" at IBM in the process of developing new computers. If you read Tracy Kidder's *Soul of the New Machine* about Data General, you find the same kind of thing in the development of their computers. It is messy, but it seems to work.

The other message that came out as we looked around these companies was that they just seemed different somehow, and we had trouble putting our finger on what was different. Suddenly we realized it was the degree to which people were running around doing things. There weren't as many committees, there weren't as many walls between offices. There were more people out in the halls running around doing things. So one message is the host of action devices to get around the bureaucratic weed patch. Maybe it's an organizational analog of entropy in physics where things sort of tend toward bureaucratic systems and you need some action devices to weed that stuff out and get on with it.

So we find Procter & Gamble insisting on one-page memos for communicating. I had lunch with a P & G brand manager, and I asked, "Is this one-page memo stuff really true?" And he said, "Well, it waxes and wanes, but I just finished a memo on a really major brand decision. It was one and a quarter pages long and it was kicked back because it was too long.

"MBWA" is a sign we first encountered at Hewlett-Packard, and then a concept we encountered everywhere—management by wandering around. Hewlett-Packard had signs like this, and they encourage it. They started to look around, looked at the way Eddie Carlson revitalized United Airlines when he was in charge. He actually used the same initials, although "management by walking about" was his phrase for it. He insisted that he and his managers spend about 60 percent of their time in the field, talking to people down at the lower levels to get ideas. That's very Japanese, incidentally. That's the source of a lot of Japanese productivity gains.

Andrall Pearson, who is the chief operating officer and president of PepsiCo, said in a recent panel, "I've probably visited more grocery stores than any of you." When he lands in a city, he goes out and visits grocery stores. That's his form of wandering about. Gerry Mitchell, who now runs Dana, says the top of the organization has to talk to the bottom directly. You find all sorts of things getting done because the top of the organization has gotten out of its ivory tower and is talking to the bottom, talking to the field, getting a good visceral impression of what's really happening down there.

Why does that make sense and how do they have time to do it? And if they do it, do they get a scientifically accurate sample? Something appears to be wrong with that process. But it isn't, really, if you look at something called patterns—or vocabularies.

If you sit and think about it—and particularly if you read the recent research in getting computers to behave like people, especially in playing games like checkers and chess—you start to see what's going on. What the artificial intelligence researchers are finding, which helps their programming out a lot, is that people tend to think in patterns. Therefore, the chess master has what Herb Simon calls a vocabulary of 50,000 chess patterns, and the class A player may have a vocabulary of maybe 2,000 to 5,000.

In my mind that's an exact analog of experience in business. What it means is that you don't have to go through all the branches on a decision tree to make a good decision. If you are experienced, you can wander about and sense opportunity or smell trouble before it occurs and certainly before it shows up in the official reports of the management information system.

I can do that in consulting. I can do that with a lot of my clients. I can go out to most McKinsey offices and I can tell you if there's trouble brewing, or I can tell you if we are on a roll. I know it long before our younger, more analytic types really sense it or else they are embarrassed to say it because they don't have the experience base. Well, what's going on for me? I've got all of these patterns.

One of my hobbies is oil painting, and so I go off with some really good oil painters once or twice a year as a way of learning. These guys claim there aren't any tricks. And then they go "swoop" and there's something great on the canvas. I ask how they did it and they say it just felt right. What's happened is that they've practiced for many years. When they first started practicing they were very careful about it. Now it's all ingrained and they just do it instinctively.

Management by wandering about, action devices, lots of task forces—that's what you find in these successful companies. Alvin Toffler brought that concept to the fore in *Future Shock.* So did Warren Bennis in a book called *The Temporary Society.* They talked about the importance of the adhocracy as the environments change rapidly. According to Toffler and Bennis, the right form of organization for issues that cut across organizational lines or fall between organizational cracks seems to be the adhocracy. A common name for that concept is the task force—not a committee but a full-time group thrown together to solve a particular issue.

The difference in the excellent companies is not the recognition of the importance of task forces because everybody has task forces. But here again is a contrast. One of our clients, when we asked to see what was being done with task forces, said, "here are the last ones we've charted in maybe the last five or six years." Out came a list of over 300 task forces. And not one of those had finished its work, not one had ever been killed. And there's the difference. What they've got are a lot of on-paper committees but certainly not what Toffler or Bennis meant by task forces.

The excellent companies, we found, know the real difference. Somebody at Digital Equipment told us the people they want on task forces are the people who are too busy to be on task forces and whose main motivation is to get the job done and get off.

What's the value of even institutional or "real" task forces? The value is that they are action devices. Small groups already are meeting, as in the estimated 9,000 quality circles at Texas Instruments called "PIP teams." PIP stands for "People Improvement Programs." They are small groups meeting to get something done. They write their own charter, they do something, they report back on what they've done, then they go on and do something else.

Or look at giant versions of the same thing as in GM's Project Center. As much trouble as the U.S. auto makers have had with the Japanese, it's impressive whenever a $60 billion corporation is able to do something. And you know, GM did it. They downsized their automobiles well ahead of their competition and they did it with a task force on a grand scale called a Project Center. Another action device.

One thing that really intrigued us in our research was the extent to which these companies experiment. Experimentation seemed to be the norm with regard to a lot of things happening inside these companies. There seemed to be a real difference again between those who were studying everything, and those who have the forthrightness to go ahead and *try* something.

The difference, in my mind, is that we seem to have learned one of the lessons from scientific management and not the other. That is, we learned the importance of analyzing and studying things, which is what I do for a living. But what we didn't learn is to experiment when there aren't good data. That's what you do as a scientist. So you listen to, for example, the transistor's inventor. He said, "I lean more to being a believer in low cunning and expediency. How do you go about starting a job? You have people who read everything; they don't get anywhere. And the people who read nothing—they don't get anywhere either. There are the people who go around asking everybody, and the people who ask nobody. I say to my own people, 'I don't know how to start a project. Why don't you step out and do an experiment?' You see, there's only one principle here. You don't first start on something which is going to take six man-months before you get to an answer. You can always find something in which, in a few hours of effort, you will have made some little steps."

On a grander example, Procter & Gamble tests and tests and tests. There are no strategic surprises here. You can see them coming for years. But you know that when they arrive it is probably time for you to move to another niche, not get in their way. They leave no stone unturned, no variable untested.

Another kind of experimentation is market testing. We first ran into it reading about a conference on innovation and growth in which Peter Peterson, then president of Bell & Howell, was a participant. The subject was zoom lenses. Peterson said he had always thought of the zoom lens as an extraordinarily expensive device, something you only use for sports events. Then one day he was in Bell & Howell's lab and saw a zoom lens. And so he asked a scientist, "What would it cost to put one on a camera?" And he said, you mean just one? Well, he supposed they could do it for about $500. Peterson said, "Well, suppose you do that because my rates are pretty high and it is going to cost more than that for us to keep talking." So they did it. Peterson said, "I did this very sophisticated piece of market research. I put it on my piano and had people by for a dinner party and they looked through it and they said, 'My, this is extraordinary. It is wonderful.' " It is very impressive if you haven't seen one before. And he said, "We did this bit of consumer research for about $500." If more industry would experiment on a low-cost basis, perhaps managements' ideas about what the market will bear would go up dramatically.

Consider Fletcher Byrom's tenth commandment at Koppers. He said, "I encourage my people to make plenty of mistakes," and then he reemphasizes, "That's right, make plenty of mistakes." That's what the small companies are forced to do that the big companies aren't doing. Somehow or the other, when you grow and become successful, you get cautious, and your tolerance for mistakes seems to go down.

Andy Pearson at PepsiCo made a supporting observation when he said the difference between a strategy that works and one that really never gets beyond paper is feedback. You get something out there and see if it works. If you do it on a small scale, you don't have to build a factory or commit yourself to $100 million. When we were giving a presentation like this a couple of years ago, somebody stepped up from one of the local power companies and he said, "I want to tell you that big plants are terrific." We thought he was going to object to everything we had said about smallness, but he added "when they work." He said, "Our problem is that they are shut down too much of the time." Same concept.

Finally, let's consider the importance of what we call the "champion." Research on innovation and growth in the excellent companies shows that they single out the importance of a champion in getting things done. And who's the champion? Well, the champion is this irrational character who hasn't done his discounted cash flows, who probably has trouble writing down a concept, but who's willing to push it through the system and make it work.

One typical champion is Howard Head, who invented the metal ski. "When I took up skiing," he said, "I had real troubles with it." He said, "Naturally I figured it was the equipment." Head is an aeronautical engineer and he's used to making things lighter and stiffer, and he thought he could do that with a ski. So he puts together this metal sandwich ski construction, goes out and tries it, and it falls apart, doesn't work. He builds other models and has ski instructors try them, but they don't work either. He goes through about forty different skis and by that time any rational person would have said, "This isn't going to work." Finally, after three agonizing winters of making refinements to the skis, they work! And boom, a whole new industry is created and it's been going ever since.

Head did the same thing with a tennis racket. He mastered skiing apparently and then he went out and he took up tennis, but he wasn't too good at that either. A lot of times when he hit the ball, the racket would twist in his hand. He said, "The equipment shouldn't do that." So he thought about it and decided that the problem was that the racket didn't have a big enough angular moment of inertia. It's like a figure skater; when she holds her hands out, she spins slower. So he widens the racket to give it a bigger angular moment of inertia so it won't twist. That has the effect of increasing the sweet spot, and another industry is off the ground.

That's not a very rational process, you see, but it takes somebody with that real belief, that vision and ability to integrate technology in the market to make it happen. So behind all of these innovations you find the role of the champion.

What we were finding when we looked at these companies wasn't only lots and lots of champions, but whole support systems for champions. I think 3M is our best model of this because it seems to be a company that is built on champions. It has introduced something like 45,000 products.

Here's a good example. A 3M employee who'd been told he had spent too much time and money on reflective sheeting came back four nights a week on his own time, without pay, to keep working on the project. What did that result in eventually? Their Scotch-Lite technology, now a major part of their business.

Tait Elder, who was heading the new ventures division of 3M at the time of our study, said, "You want systems that really control the excesses because you can't experiment on a grand scale. If you are Boeing, for instance, you don't want airplanes falling out of the sky. You want some control in the system, but at the same time you want leaky systems so that people will be able to scrounge." Somebody from IBM who had been around since founder Tom Watson's days said, "I judge the creative health of an organization by the amount of scrounging that's going on." One sees in these companies not only an understanding of champions but all kinds of support systems for champions.

At 3M, if you can't get a product approved through your own division or group, it is perfectly okay to take it to somebody else's group or division, or you can take it to new ventures, or to the president. At the time we did the study anyway, people were actually rewarded for the number of products they'd sponsored from other divisions and groups. Now that's part of the compensation system.

You see the principle here. It's a numbers game on new products and innovation and development. You don't know what's going to work. No amount of planning is going to tell you what's going to work. You get enough things out there, make plenty of mistakes, let people try things even if they initially fail, and—by sheer numbers—you get innovative success.

Another fascinating support system we found was the use of Fellows programs in organizations. At Texas Instruments or IBM they talk a lot about their Fellows programs. Basically, these are people in the system who have been given a budget to go around supporting ideas. Initially the idea, at least at TI, was that if anybody had a super idea, he or she could take it to the president. That was a little bit formidable, so they commissioned about 123 Individual Contributors, so anybody with an idea could take it to a Contributor. He or she could sponsor an idea up to a certain budget level, and then go forward with the idea. TI's Speak and Spell system came out of that.

These programs sounded like such a nifty idea that we tried it with one of our clients who was having real problems. Their strategy called for lots more in the way of product line extensions. So we said, among other things, "Why don't you try a Fellows program?" They did it with some trepidation, and we had some, too. They set up a budget of $250,000, five Fellows with $50,000 apiece. What they were supposed to do in the system was to sponsor anybody who had an idea that they felt was good. So these five Fellows were able to sponsor projects they considered worthwhile.

Since then, what's come up through the Fellows program in terms of commercially successful ideas and innovations has outstripped what's come up through the normal R & D channels by a factor of about 5 to 1. They've already got a couple of cost-saving ideas that combined are worth $2.5 million annually. They got that for a budget of $250,000 a year. Another major attribute of these companies is that they are close to the customer. When I went to business school in 1960, Theodore Levitt had just written a book on marketing excellence. He said you've got to be close to the customer and you've got to innovate and all the same things we're saying right now. So what's new? It's the fanaticism and the high energy with which these companies pursue customer service. It's Frito-Lay with 10,000 salesmen running around peddling potato chips and corn chips, and their whole notion of themselves is that they call on a customer, big, medium, or small, once every 24 hours. Any analyst is going to come in and tell you that's wrong, that you'll save a lot of money by reducing the number of visits and people will never know the difference. But then you see the market share figures. They are terrific, 60 and 70 percent, and you suddenly realize there's some magic there.

These companies are service fanatics. IBM has classic ideas about service. What do you buy when you buy IBM? You don't just buy the machine. What they are really selling is the fact that if you buy this from IBM, you don't have to worry because if it breaks down they'll fix it, and if you have software problems they'll fix that. I went to work for IBM as a summer supplementary data processing trainee. After a couple of months, when I had learned my title, what did they have us trainees do? They sent us back to Endicott, New York, and taught us how to wire punch card equipment. I spent my first month installing a punch card system for a customer, and I spent my next month fixing punch card systems that had gone down, and then the last month I went out and learned something about sales. The whole idea that comes across is service. They were training me, a future salesman, about the importance of IBM and its concept of service.

On a grander level, IBM observes a practice of taking some of its top salesmen and making them assistants. What do they do? They respond to customer complaints. There's the service idea again. Ray Kroc, in a wonderful book about McDonald's titled *Grinding It Out*, says, "If I had a brick for every time I'd said the phrase 'Quality, Service, Cleanliness and Value,' I could bridge the Atlantic Ocean." It's the same thing. If you read the McDonald's annual report of last year, the first paragraph starts out with the words "Quality, Service, Cleanliness and Value," and on they go. It's the persistence of the idea. It's the overkill. It's the fanaticism with which these companies practice this closeness to the customer that struck us as being really unusual. At Caterpillar, if you as a customer can't get a part in 48 hours, you get it for free.

We, like everybody else, had been doing some research on the personal computer. Hewlett-Packard was late entering that market. But the interesting thing is that when you go out and talk to dealers and to the marketplace and ask "Who's going to survive the shakeout, with 150 different manufacturers," they mention IBM and Apple, and a lot of them mention HP. Why is that? They may have never seen an HP piece of equipment. But they say, "Because HP makes stuff that works." They expect them to be successful, because HP has a reputation for making quality stuff that works. Somehow they know or at least they believe that if HP gets in there in a big way, they are going to succeed. It's a brand franchise that people would pay millions for in consumer goods. It's astonishing.

P & G, the first to put its 800 number on packaging, got 200,000 phone calls out of that the first year. They respond to every one of those calls and report on them at the board level. They get lots of new product ideas out of that. What we felt we were observing in the customer area was another major dimension of innovation, most strikingly put forward by Eric von Hippel of MIT in a study of innovation in the scientific instruments industry. What he found was that of the 160 innovations he looked at, eleven were what he called "first of type" innovations. All eleven—100 percent—had been first invented, prototyped, and tested in customer labs. All of those inventions essentially came from the customer. Of the sixty-six major improvements he looked at, 85 percent had come from the customer. Of eighty-three "minor" improvements, about two-thirds came from users.

That's probably an extreme example, because if you talk to Boeing or to Raychem or some of the others who see themselves as more technically driven, what you quickly find is what I refer to as tight coupling between the technology and the market. Boeing says, "Look, if we don't test our new idea in the market pretty fast, it doesn't go much further."

And you talk to Raychem, which prides itself on doing things nobody else can do technologically. That's the way they find new markets and new opportunities. They go out and look for something that is really hard to do technically. And if they feel that it's fairly easy to do technically or that somebody else has already done it, they won't do it. They are always in the forefront of technology, but they are very quick to tell you that the way they sell is by offering phenomenal levels of customer service. They say, "Look, we're always asking our customers to be pioneers, so the only way we can sell what we develop is to offer unusual care for the customer."

When a company is doing that, what do you get? In my mind, you get a certain pride in what the company is doing, which introduces the productivity and people question. What we observed as we went around were largely nonunion, reasonably happy work forces that had a lot of respect for the companies. What you are generating with these companies is not only quality, service, and reliability but also real respect because employees are proud of what their companies do.

A long time ago I read *Working* by Studs Terkel. I was kind of fascinated with it. Who were the happiest workers? Well, they tended to be the stonemasons and people like that who could identify with their work. They could look back and see this thing they had built, and they felt proud of it. They could identify. If a company is doing what I assert these excellent companies are doing, people can identify with their work because they are proud of what they are producing or offering.

I'm just fascinated when I talk to ex-McDonald's employees because a lot of the work they did is strictly Dullsville. But they tell me, "It's a funny thing, but when I go out for an inexpensive hamburger, I go back to McDonald's." That's hard for me to imagine, because if I worked as long as some of them had for any establishment, I think I would be sick of the place and wouldn't go back there. They go back to McDonald's, however. Somehow they are still proud of what that company stands for. And on a grander scale you see that with the other companies.

Now let's look at productivity in people. In 1942, Allen H. Mogensen said, "The person doing the job knows far better than anyone else the best way of doing that job and, therefore, is the best one fitted to improve it." Who is this guy? He ran seminars in the 1920–1940s in Lake Placid, N.Y. on work simplification (now rediscovered as "job enrichment") and in 1942 published an article in *Fortune* preaching productivity. He was out of the same school as W. Edwards Demming, who taught the Japanese most of what they now know about productivity. In fact, there's a Demming prize in Japan and Hewlett-Packard just won it. It's a prize for quality. They are very proud of it; quality and productivity *do* go together. So there are people around who have been preaching this theme for years, and a few have taken it seriously. That's the good news. Most of us haven't, which is the bad news.

Rene McPherson, now at Stanford, makes a statement hauntingly similar to Mogensen. He says, "Until we believe the expert in any job is the person performing it, we shall forever limit the potential of that person. Consider a manufacturing setting. Within their 25-foot area, nobody knows more about how to operate a machine, improve its quality, optimize the material flow or keep it operating than the machine operators. Nobody."

Kimsey Mann, who ran Blue Bell, a highly successful company Number Two behind Levi Strauss in the apparel business, says essentially the same thing. Who knows the job better than those close to it?

We find management in these companies practicing MBWA and getting out talking to the employees, getting lots of employee ideas, and really treating the individuals with respect. The chairman of Marks and Spencer once was asked to talk on industrial relationships and when he got to the podium he had fury in his eyes. He said, "I'm asked to talk about industrial relationships." He said, "I'm not going to talk about industrial relationships. I don't know any industrials. I'm going to talk about people." Teaching with Rene McPherson at Stanford, we had hauled out an ad from one of the companies talking about its efforts in something like "industrial relationships." McPherson ripped it up in front of the class. He said, "It never talks about people. The word 'people' isn't in there."

So the concept comes across. They treat people as adults in these better organizations. They are not industrials, they are not second-class citizens, they are people. And that message is reinforced.

IBM's philosophy is largely contained in simple beliefs. As Tom Watson, Jr., put it in *A Business and Its Beliefs:* "I want to begin with what I think is the most important [belief]. A respect for the individual. This is a simple concept, but in IBM it occupies a major portion of management time. We devote more effort to it than anything else." If you look at Bill Hewlett's words in a document called the HP Way, you find that exact same phrase: respect for the individual.

One reason the Japanese are as successful as they are is they seem to understand that concept and are practicing it in their own way. An interesting example is Toyota Motors. In 1976 Toyota started that most sophisticated of all management tools, the suggestion system. When they started it they had about 10,000 suggestions coming in from all over. By 1978 they had hiked it in Japanese fashion and had over a million suggestions coming in. And they had taken an estimated $250 million annually out of their cost base as a result of those suggestions. They were receiving eighteen suggestions per worker per year as compared with, as far as we can tell, one for every three workers per year at General Motors—an enormous difference.

We found unusual numbers of reward systems in these companies. They weren't just monetary rewards, but lots and lots of reward systems all the way from gold stars to gas barbecue prizes. Lots of hoopla, and lots of reward systems.

Again, the question is, what's going on in these companies? It relates back to some reading we'd done in psychology research where groups of people were asked to rank themselves in terms of various things such as athletic ability. Sixty percent put themselves in the top quartile. People were asked to rank themselves in terms of ability to get along with one another and the numbers were even higher. What does that tell you? That tells you that our self-image is pretty high, and that we basically like reward systems. Where you have lots of hoopla and lots of reward systems, whether it is gold stars or gold bananas or bonus systems that reinforce the notion of ourselves as winners, we think you get a lot more out of people. We see the contrast in some of our clients that have bonus systems that pay out only 50 percent of the time, where you have few reward systems. You are defining a lot of people as losers, and that's not consistent with their self-image. They don't like that.

A marvelous example is Delta's Productivity in People theme. They encourage the Family Feeling; they really practice it. On a trip to Atlanta, I asked a flight attendant, "Did you really buy the company an airplane?" She got a little choked up about the story; and she described how it rolled across the tarmac all festooned with red ribbons. I said, "Well, why did you do it?" She said, "Well, we're so happy that they would adopt a policy of no layoffs, and no salary cuts, that we felt we owed the company something." And so they got together and bought Delta a $30 million airplane. Others talk about how Delta survived the 1973–1974 oil crisis with over 200 pilots working at handling and loading baggage instead of being laid off. Today many of them are on voluntary leave, but their benefits continue. So the stories go on.

Most excellent companies seem to know what they stand for, and they seem to be managers of their own value systems. Any company is going to be a creature of its value systems. Any group of people that have been together develop shared values, whether they want to or not. Those value systems can either be pretty healthy or they can be very unhealthy.

We did a lot of internal training and we asked groups that came into our workshops to rate companies on certain performance measures. Then we compared it with their shared value systems and we found a dramatic difference between companies that talked not of their superordinate goals, but only of earnings value. Those companies that really did have a rich set of superordinate goals talked about people and they talked about the people in the marketplace. The difference was that companies with the much richer set of values were performing far better, both in terms of growth and in terms of earnings, than the ones that had only financial objectives. The difference was striking. I'm sure that if we probe that further, we'll find it's even more true than the initial research.

Changing a company's value system takes real obsession from the top few managers over a period of years, not months. But that is what leadership is all about. And if we have more managers who are really leading by doing, particularly by paying attention to the value systems of the organization, I think that we in America needn't worry too much about growth.

INDUSTRIES TO ACCOMMODATE AN EXPANDING
II. POPULATION

Gene D. Sullivan, Moderator

When you start looking at the ingredients that go into growth, you quickly find that the human element is a critical one. People—in their multiple roles as consumers, homemakers, and business people—form the markets for our nation's industries.

Growth opportunities can be rare in a stagnating region where the population is holding stable, or even declining. That has been the unhappy experience of some states in the upper Midwest tied to traditional "smokestack" industries.

On the other hand, the Sunbelt states of the South and the Southwest have been fueled by a steady stream of migrants from less temperate climes. Since World War II, states such as Florida and California and Georgia have been stimulated by an influx of families—and of businesses shifting southward or westward to serve them.

Let's look at some of the opportunities created by population growth, and some industries whose ability to serve growing populations has helped them to flourish.

Our first contributor, Walter A. Forbes, will provide some insight into the new wave in retailing. Forbes, vice chairman and chief executive officer of Comp-U-Card of America, will discuss the impact of computerized shopping, an area that his firm has pioneered. Comp-U-Card is an innovative mail-order retailing firm based in Stamford, Connecticut.

Ray Stevenson will review new business opportunities emerging in medical services. Ray has an excellent perspective on the subject as president of Charter Medical Corporation of Macon, Georgia, a $400 million firm providing medical services to burgeoning popula-

tion centers in fifteen states. Charter also operates health care facilities in England, Saudi Arabia, and Puerto Rico.

Next will be Howard Katz, the president of Ocilla Industries, another fast-growing firm. He will bring us his viewpoint on construction and the evolution of our traditional family home. Ocilla, which specializes in manufactured or modular housing, has done well by providing housing to families that, because of high construction and mortgage costs, have been effectively shut out of the market for several years.

Concluding this section will be the Atlanta Fed's Donald Koch, who will address the question of how to change the corporate culture through information systems. Don, who was named two years ago as the Bank's director of research, will detail his experience guiding the Research Department's reorganization into a highly productive unit that relies heavily on electronics.

Together, these presentations should provide us with a new look at the type of industries that have been created, or have expanded, to accommodate the "Baby Boomers" who are moving into their most productive earning—and consuming—years.

WALTER A. FORBES

Retailing: The Impact of Computerized Shopping

We certainly believe we are pioneering a major growth business that will have an effect on all of us and will radically change a common basic function of our lives—shopping. I want to speculate now on the future of retailing without stores, without paper, without print, without catalogs—nothing, all electronic.

Since the early 1950s, science fiction writers and futurists have been speculating on how our lives would be in the 1980s and 1990s. In their speculations, they usually refer to the computer as being the basic change agent. And while some of the dreams haven't happened—we don't have robots in our homes yet—a lot of what they forecast has really been exceeded today.

We believe that people's needs and desires don't really change. What changes, what will always continue to change, is how we fulfill those needs and desires. We may be banking, for instance, at an automatic banking teller, but we still have trouble balancing our checkbook. We may shop at a supermarket and use the debit card that puts our money into the supermarket instantly, but that doesn't really affect our feelings about the prices of products within that supermarket. It's still shocking. We still have problems making ends meet.

We are living in an age where we are learning to marry the needs of everyday existence to the exciting products that technology gives us. One of the most promising areas is the emergence of electronic retailing. Yet many if not most in the retail field, despite seeing how technology has changed most other businesses, seem to be ignoring the change that it would bring to their own business.

As with any new development and the way people live and do business, it's difficult, perhaps impossible, to predict the eventual size and shape of this newest form of retailing. I'll use our company, Comp-U-Card, as a case example.

Retailing itself is an evolutionary process. It's a vibrant and dynamic business that has to adapt constantly to changing consumer patterns. Electronic retailing, however, represents more than just another minor change in the retailing process. The retailer's savings on space, inventory, employee costs, and capital investments and the price convenience, simplicity, and range of merchandise made available to the consumer by electronic retailing give it the potential to be the most revolutionary development in how we conduct our basic trade since we went to money.

This change is different from a new kind of store, a new location for a store, up-size for a store or down-size. Direct selling is already with us. Depending on whom you believe, in 1980 there were over $110 billion worth of direct sales. Over $9 billion was spent on direct telephone marketing in 1982.

An estimated 85 percent of the adult population has ordered either by mail or telephone at least once in the last twelve months. This is the foundation that electronic retailing is going to build from. It's still difficult to anticipate the eventual size of the electronic marketplace, but the potential is enormous. T. Rowe Price is talking about a 20-percent growth rate. In our computer shopping business, we have been maintaining for almost two years a 20-percent growth rate every month in our product sales.

The only way you can get into the Comp-U-Card system right now is through one of the computer utilities. Our shopping service under various names is available from The Source or from Compuserve. It's on Dow Jones' information retrieval system. We are also on interactive cable with Times Mirror. We are involved, I believe, with every major interactive banking test that is being contemplated.

So I think it's fair to say that, at the moment, we have a 100-percent share of the market. We know of no other interactive shopping service. People who use this service have access to over 50,000 name-brand products directly from their home or office. For example, in looking at what people were buying on the computer we found that in one week we sold stereos, VCRs, TVs, miscellaneous video, phones, phone equipment, refrigerators, clothes, cameras, portable stereos, washers, microwaves, vacuums, automobiles, crystal, silver, and china.

That is just where we are today. Before long, we'll begin to introduce financial services, pharmaceuticals, certain food items, travel, and insurance. I think it will only take us a couple of years to increase our basic products to over 200,000.

This data base is going to have a major effect on a lot of traditional sectors of our economy. In total we now have 2 million people who are members of our system. It costs $25 a year for an individual to access this system. These are people not only interested in shopping, but they're paying to shop.

These 2 million people use our data base to purchase products. Let's look at a representative group, trying to put a few numbers on a business where there are no numbers. I looked at 1,000 computer shoppers as a random sample and found out the following things, reviewing their activity over the past year. The average order placed over our system was $300. The average shopping time was approaching an hour a month on the computer, and that also is growing rapidly.

People are buying at least once a year and many four or five times a year. And over 25 percent of the people who have our service use it every month. Many times they use it just for information. But, again, they not only had to pay to join the service, they are paying the usage charge to come in and get our information. You can see that this is a data base that apparently has real value to the consumer.

As people shop, this computer terminal becomes more and more a part of their everyday lives. Besides making purchases, our users can be involved in electronic auctions. We have daily and weekly auctions where you can come in and bid against others to get products.

They can participate in product information searches, play product games, exchange consumer information, or call through any terminal. I'm not talking even about a home computer, although that would work; any terminal of any kind will come into our system.

Thinking about how this is going to grow, we expect that banks, telephone companies, cable companies, brokerage houses, and others will realize before long that it makes sense for them to give you a terminal if you don't already have one or else lease it to you very economically.

Once this very large data base is accessible in every home, a traditional retailer will suddenly wake up and find a competitor never before considered. It's not going to be someone just in the area. It's going to be a nationwide type of competitor.

When you join our system you have access to our data base and, as a home terminal user, you can design a product feature-by-feature. For instance, you don't have to know what you want. You can say that you would like to buy a television set and the computer will ask you all the features questions, since every item in our data base is coded that way. So you literally design what you want, say what you want to spend— and the computer will give you every single alternative in that category sold in the United States.

For instance, we carry every single brand-name television and every single model in everybody's line. You have total accessibility to the entire U.S. marketplace.

You have the ability in our system to compare prices across specific model numbers so that you can see what a real price is, because our information is not static. If you want it, you can buy it. That's a real price. It's a meaningful price, a competitive price.

You can get detailed descriptions of individual items so you know exactly what you are buying. You can place an order electronically, pay by credit card or check, and arrange for delivery into your home anywhere in the United States.

In addition, because of the economics of this computer system, it will cost you, in general, 10 to 40 percent less than the best price in your marketplace—not just your department store, but better than a discount store. Think about our system for a minute. It's on 24 hours a day, seven days a week. When people come in and shop at midnight, there is not even a light bulb burning in our company, much less a person on payroll.

There are no bricks, no mortar. It's just a data base. The more it gets used, the more efficient it is. Therefore, the pricing that this sort of electronic retailing can give, on top of all the other advantages such as convenience, make it a phenomenally tough competitor for a person in the traditional retail business.

I want to point out that convenience is also a major factor in our favor; with up to 50 percent of all married women working, with such a high percentage of families that have a single head of household, the time savings offered by our shop-at-home service assume an even greater importance.

Other trends likely to help us include the high cost of shopping and operating a car, parking, the rise in public transportation costs, the lack of salespeople with any product knowledge, the lack of salespeople at all, the desire for more leisure time in many cities and, sadly, the fear of crime. All of these things encourage people to shop from home.

I don't think that many of those trends are going to be reversed in the near term. I think when you take all those conveniences and the price factor as well, it's easy to see why a company like ours is growing so rapidly.

Let me point out that this is done with just alphanumeric terminals, without a sales pitch or advertising support. All that our system has is information and the ability to order. That is the state of the art in the home today.

While this development might be considered revolutionary, retailing itself is more evolutionary, so this isn't going to happen overnight. Another development will occur very rapidly and this is what we call the electronics store.

We're putting out this product called Comp-U-Store that will take advantage of our mainframe computer. We are going to add interactive video to the system, so we have the audiovisual power of television as well as the information that powers our mainframe computer. The emergence of this method of electronic retailing holds promise for retailers and consumers.

We can, in less than twenty square feet, put one of our electronic stores in and sell 50,000 to 100,000 items, without any inventory investment on the part of the store.

Suddenly, retailers can literally enter into any market they choose. If a retailer feels that a nearby camera store is hurting its product mix, we can install a camera store in literally an hour that will offer more products at better prices than the competition.

Clearly, with the power of television, you can sell. You can put people on to certain products. You can explain their various features.

We expect to have seven or eight of these Comp-U-Stores out in a month and, according to our present projections, we will have more than 3,000 units in about five years. The market is there. To date, we have not seen any reason why this type of retailing shouldn't grow dramatically over the next few years. There are just too many arguments in favor of this sort of process.

Let me describe this store a bit because it has some pretty interesting features. For instance, in the alphanumeric system, you must have some concept of how to push a button and answer the computer's questions. But with a video disc, the way we've engineered it, you can leaf through the electronics catalog just in pictures first, stop at the product you want, and then go back to the alphanumeric information. It has a card reader so you can put your credit card through and it can identify you and make the transaction.

We'll soon be able to print you not just a regular receipt, but we'll print you a colored picture of the item. When you go home you can show whomever you wish exactly the item you are getting. With our partners in both Japan and Europe, we're working now so that in three to four or five years this terminal will actually be able to talk to you and you to it, not unlike a salesperson today. The advantage is that, when you talk to this computer, it knows everything about the product you want and is perfectly trained.

Again, in this sort of retail system, you don't have to do preliminary shopping because you can design the features. You can literally imagine a product and, if it exists, the computer will tell you who has it, what manufacturer makes it, and at what price.

If you think for a minute of the effect of a Comp-U-Store on your home shopping, you can see how electronic marketing will begin to affect the retail structure. A Comp-U-Store can eliminate the middleman between manufacturer and consumer. Various levels of wholesalers and distributors may have to find other services to provide because surely, if all this comes to pass, they're going to lose market share.

Either that or they're going to have to develop the ability to sell directly into the consumer's home. There simply will be no reason for a manufacturer to issue a product and deliver it to the store and then to a home. We're essentially by-passing all of this.

I think the refinements in merchandising techniques afforded by a

Comp-U-Store retail terminal will provide consumers with more information, more selection, fashion advice, service, advertising—things you simply can't get in retailing today.

So what we are saying is that retailers have an interesting long-term problem. Those that don't attempt to adapt to the electronic method of doing business are really going to find themselves at both a price and a service disadvantage, fighting in many retail categories to stay in business.

We are not saying that stores will disappear, that a department store that has fashion excitement like a Bloomingdale's is really in danger. But we are saying that in five to ten years, you're not going to be able to go to an appliance store. It simply won't be there. There won't be any need for it.

Certainly manufacturers are already having difficulty finding people who want to carry a bulky and expensive product like a refrigerator. There is really no reason for that in the electronic marketplace. When these systems get well established, it's going to have a profound effect on how a lot of people do business—not just the retailer, but the manufacturer, the wholesaler, and the distributor.

The real prize in this whole electronic shopping thing is to put that in-store terminal in the home, to put video on demand in the home. That is the real prize for the people in our business. We have a lot of the pieces. We have the interactive terminal, we have video in our cable, and we have a shopping service program that we have experimented with. We have the laser disc in the store.

When we put that all together, we can then have a consumer who can call up any product, any type of information, right from the home. At that point, electronic shopping becomes fully competitive with all forms of catalog retailing today and basically competitive with most forms of traditional retailing. If you decide you want to buy something, you can instantly call up a picture, a demonstration, a product history, or consumer reports—and do that at a great price advantage.

The competitive power of electronic retailing has gone ahead of the basic retailer already. Our company has tremendous advantages. Unlike a store that has to handle markdowns and worry about changes in the marketplace, we can change prices in an instant. We can change an entire line of prices in a keystroke. We can add products. We can eliminate products. We can be much more responsive to the environment in our sort of system.

There are some things that electronic retailing hasn't solved yet and one of them is the foundation of traditional retailing—the spontaneous purchase. It's hard to walk by your television set and decide that you need something unless you turn it on and search for it. Somebody in the electronics area will have to find out how to create that equivalent of a spontaneous sale. It may be in cable, with some sort of entertaining television program, but it's most likely that innovation will come from all the data.

When you're hooked into a home and the resident is shopping through your system, that system can capture a tremendous amount of information. You can know how long a person looked at a product by brand and whether or not it was bought. Somewhere in all that information the electronic retailer is going to possess, there will probably be a way to figure out how to make spontaneous sales.

Since every single terminal on our system can be addressed differently, you can begin to build special data bases for that particular home that has an interest in a particular product. If the family happens to be into coin collecting, you could put coin-collecting opportunities in front of them. You could also price every terminal differently.

In any case, I think the jump from today's alphanumeric terminals to this multimedia video-based terminal, is going to be a major revolutionary breakthrough. And it's not that far off. We think we will have that system in many homes in five years. I would like to believe we'll be the only one doing that, but I'm pretty sure we won't be. The IBMs of the world, the AT&Ts of the world, and others have seen what we are doing and are going to come at this business with in-store terminals and in-home videos on demand.

This is going to happen quickly. It started about five years ago. We are only five years away from having that in place, in numbers. I think that this interactive video system, if we want to really speculate about the future, can lead to an interesting retail system.

If you think about our retailing system and manufacturers' problems, take refrigerators, for example, there is no reason why you can't eventually have the consumer tied directly into the manufacturer. In a sense, you're designing the refrigerator you want and sending your order to the manufacturer, who sends it to you.

When you think about that system, and all the people it leaves out of the system, then you're going to see some dramatic changes in the retail structure in this country. Based on the way people use our terminal, we see no reason why it can't happen.

In ten years, I don't think you will be able to go out and find someone who would stock more than a sample refrigerator. It just isn't going to be economical to keep more of an inventory.

By 1990 we expect that 25 percent of all households—and this is without any major player like the phone company coming in and giving everybody a terminal—will have a terminal that can call up our data base and others. We conducted a little experiment in six cities on cable just to see the effect of introducing a shopping channel. So we began a program that was on seven days a week for about fourteen hours a day. It had nothing to do but talk about products, pretty boring stuff.

We tried to make it interesting, but we have not found a way to do that yet. In any case, we ran it for just sixty days. We did not promote it, yet the average purchase came out to a projected $600 a year for people who had access to that system. Six hundred dollars a year.

If you think about all the people who have terminals and you start multiplying that $600, you are talking about hundreds of billions of dollars.

I can't prove how big that number will be, but that test was limited to consumer durables. We have not really even begun to get into the high-volume items. We're starting to get into clothes now, but we have not gotten into consumables like foods and others. So there is an immense potential to disrupt traditional channels of distribution and swing consumers over to the electronic side.

Once you have this pipeline into the house, you can begin to put a lot of other services down that line. For some months we have been issuing our own Visa cards as one of our first financial services. We are going into the IRA business, the money fund business, travel, and insurance.

You can start affecting other businesses. There is really no reason why you have to deal from anywhere other than your home to buy insurance. In fact, some of our computer programs might be more understandable to the purchaser of insurance than listening to the average agent. If you combine all that, it's going to take a big piece of business from somewhere.

What we're suggesting to everyone thinking about the future is that if you're in that pipeline somewhere where we're going to be taking some business away, you had better take a look at electronic selling sooner rather than later because we're growing as rapidly as we possibly can. And we are just the first company.

Comp-U-Card is a company that is taking every risk possible, trying to preempt every market, growing way too fast because we won't be able to do it much longer before we get real competition. Some problems might arise from this type of selling. There is the danger of the misuse of information that a service like ours can gather. Those of us pioneering in this field aren't unaware of some of those problems, such as whether you would want someone to know that you just spent an hour looking at a catalog of X-rated movies. That sort of danger of misuse exists, and clearly, if we want to make this as big a business as we'd like, we're going to have to deal with that.

We have 2 million members today although we have never done any advertising of any kind. Last year, we contacted only 500,000 homes and told them about our service. This year, we are contacting 10 million credit-worthy homes, telling them about our service, our Visa program, offering them the chance to buy through our system either on the phone or through their own computer terminal.

That sort of growth is going to make a difference in our effect on the marketplace. I emphasize again that we're only the first company. We are extremely lucky at the moment. No one else is doing it, but we are aware of at least five or six others interested in getting into this business that have assets 100 times more than ours.

Whether you are a retailer, service company, manufacturer, or a bank, it doesn't matter, you are going to be affected. What it's going to mean for all of us is that there are going to be some wonderful opportunities to invest in some of the emerging companies in this business. On the other hand, there probably will be some good opportunities to sell short in some of the traditional companies that lack vision.

Let me explain how you can go into our system and shop. The computer will generate a quick summary of the major categories of product. Within the general category of television, for example, it lists all the various subcategories of product that we carry in the system. It will ask for a brand name. If you know what you are shopping for, you could get an instant price. If you have no preference on brand it will ask if you want color or black and white. Let's say you want a color set. The obvious next question is screen size. Say you're looking for a 19-inch. It's now going to ask how much you want to spend. It doesn't want to waste your time listing every remote television. Say you don't want to spend too much. It will tell you that there are two pages of television sets that meet those simple criteria.

If you think about a data base, it's really running a commodities market of consumer durable goods. The computer can come up with a fully delivered cost to your home.

On every product, you can get further information—what it lists for, what our cost is, what the savings are—and it asks if you want to order. It could give you a picture of that set. If you wanted to order, you would just go through a simple order form. It would issue a specific order number to you, and tell you when the set was going to show up at your house.

Once you have this in your house, it becomes narcotic. It's unlikely that you would go shopping without checking on this system.

RAY STEVENSON

Medical Services: Contributions to Growth

The first hospital in the Western Hemisphere was established by the Spanish in 1503 in what is now the Dominican Republic. Two hundred years before Christ, Buddhists in India started the predecessors of to-day's hospitals. How can it be that, twenty-four centuries after Hippo-crates, hospitals suddenly have emerged as a growth industry?

It is not difficult to understand why new medical technologies and new wonder drugs have created tremendous opportunities for companies in the health care field. The income statements of such companies re-flect the classic growth characteristics of heavy research and develop-ment spending and aggressive sales and marketing efforts.

Although they also stand to benefit from advances in medical tech-nologies, hospitals are different. Their basic business of providing a rel-atively uncomplicated physical plant in which a physician can treat a patient has not changed significantly for at least a hundred years.

What factors, then, are responsible for the health care sector's grow-ing at a much faster rate than the U.S. economy as a whole? In partic-ular, why have investor-owned hospitals been one of the best-perform-ing industry groups for nearly a decade, both fundamentally and in terms of stock market acceptance?

At the risk of raising the ire of my entrepreneurial colleagues who started our industry, I am going to suggest that had it not been for Medi-care and the federal government, the hospital management industry, at least as we know it today, would not exist. In 1966, the Medicare Act validated the philosophical and political notion that, at least for a certain segment of the population, health care was a right, not a priv-ilege or a luxury.

This legislation was passed over the strenuous objections of physi-cians and other health care providers. Medicare gave the public stamp of approval to concepts of health insurance that had been gaining stronger footholds in the private sector, usually in the form of employer group medical and hospital coverage.

It is ironic that the shift of massive amounts of resources into the public sector for the Medicare program created a new entrepreneurial opportunity in the private sector. This apparent contradiction arises because of a hospital's unique social, professional, political, and economic role.

The demand for hospital admissions and associated in-patient services is mediated by physicians, not by the patients themselves. Historically, doctors have had little incentive to consider the price of treatment for insured patients. In fact, many physicians have no idea what hospital costs comprise.

Since most patients do not pay directly for their hospital care, the demand for hospital services is not very price sensitive. This situation is exacerbated in our somewhat litigious society by the threat of malpractice actions. Doctors tend to order every test in the book to protect themselves against lawsuits.

No patient has ever shown up at a hospital saying, "I want the cheapest care that you have." Until very recently, no hospital administrator ever succeeded by emphasizing expense control. Administrators' primary concerns were improving medical technology and increasing intensity of care.

In other words, Medicare was introduced into a climate where incentives to control hospital costs and to lower prices tended to be weak or nonexistent. In keeping with this cavalier attitude toward costs, Medicare was designed with no incentives for efficiency. Literally overnight, the program created an enormous demand for hospital services in an age group of the population that would continue to be among the fastest growing for decades to come.

However, Congress failed to mandate, or even to suggest, any mechanism for delivering these hospital services in a cost-effective manner. Moreover, like any government program involving many dollars, Medicare soon created a large bureaucracy whose jobs depended on the program's perpetuation. It also created a vast political contingency of beneficiaries known for their active participation at the polls.

It may be helpful to think of Medicare in the context of the Great Society. It was a time before Vietnam and Watergate, a time when politicians told the people that there was nothing the government couldn't do—and the people believed them. It was easy to ignore the possibility that the Medicare program eventually would run into trouble. However, with the benefit of seventeen years of hindsight, I believe the Medicare program's major shortcomings have not been its economic or social consequences, but its psychological effect.

In short, Medicare was responsible for solidifying the myth that health care in this country is free. The Great Society legitimized so-called free health care for the elderly. Along with expanding insurance plans in the work place, Medicare effectively insulated the consumer of health care services from reality by giving the perception that treatment wasn't costing anything out of his or her own pocket.

When approximately 90 cents of every hospital dollar is paid by someone else, you can hardly blame the health care consumer for succumbing to the illusion that hospital care is free. This fundamental distortion of the normal supply-demand equation was given added impetus by Medicare. In a typical competitive market, the quantity of a product or service demanded by consumers will decline if the price increases. Thus the survival of an enterprise depends critically on management's ability to keep costs and prices low. However, there is a strong psychological tendency to believe that health care is free, even when all statistical information clearly indicates that those costs are virtually out of control. Traditional economic relationships wither in such a psychological environment and strong incentives for management to control resource use are discarded.

In that climate, which was anything but businesslike, it took vision to recognize in the mid-1960s that there could be opportunities for someone who looked at hospitals as a business. Yet those opportunities were turned into one of America's premier growth industries during the last decade.

Why were most of the entrepreneurs who stepped forward with this vision southerners? At the time Medicare became law, most of the major medical centers in the United States were in the North. This was not coincidental; most of this country's great industrial wealth was in the North. The great philanthropists and wealthy families, religious groups, and voluntary organizations established large medical centers in their hometowns. Over the years, as these medical centers grew along with their primarily urban populations, they gave rise to an entrenched medical establishment with a rigid not-for-profit orientation.

In the South, by contrast, the population was poorer and more rural and generally did not enjoy philanthropy to the extent allowed by the great wealth of families like the Mellons, the Carnegies, and the Rockefellers. So when Medicare created a significant incremental demand for hospital care, most of the underserved areas happened to be in the Sunbelt. The region was growing rapidly anyway, and the managers of the New South were not afraid to juxtapose the words *profit* and *health care*.

These businessmen were motivated by the potential they saw for profits through efficiency and economies of scale. These profits would help form the capital required to keep the hospitals up-to-date. This was necessary to meet the constantly rising expectations of physicians and patients. The latter, especially, increasingly viewed expert care as something owed to them, with no cost of their own.

Once the companies were organized, they showed that hospitals could be managed efficiently—could earn a fair return—while still rendering excellent care. As track records of earnings were established, access to capital opened up and the companies began to develop experienced managers of their own and to attract good management from other industries. After 500 years, the entire concept of hospital management began to change.

First and foremost, professional management significantly streamlined hospital decision making by imposing clear lines of authority and accountability. Not-for-profit hospital boards are notoriously unwieldy. Their members are usually untrained in hospital administration and frequently wear other hats in the community that can conflict with their hospital duties.

The voluntary community hospitals have always been the heart of our health care system. But, with all due respect, the doctors, nurses, nuns, and Kiwanis Club members who run these institutions have not always had the savvy some of their counterparts have today. The management companies created a revolution in hospital government by eliminating or modifying these traditional structures. This revolution may prove to be one of the most significant lasting contributions the private sector will make to health care delivery.

Multihospital organizations also quickly changed the nature of health care from a kind of cottage industry to one national in scope. Broader geographic horizons enabled the management companies to meet community needs for growing regions that did not have large public-sector or voluntary health and hospital establishments. Many emerging communities prefer a viable partnership with a private-sector provider to taking on the burdens of publicly financing a large not-for-profit institution.

This trend will continue through the 1980s. Under today's more restrictive Medicare payment regulations, many not-for-profit institutions that have been operating relatively inefficiently are expected to find it increasingly difficult to keep going at the taxpayers' expense. These institutions may seek affiliation of some form with investor-owned companies such as Charter Medical.

Charter Medical added a new wrinkle to this entrepreneurial scenario. Founded by William A. Fickling, Jr., in 1969, Charter Medical started a little later and with considerably less capital than the major companies in the general acute-care management industry. In addition, the company owned some nursing homes and other properties unrelated to its small core of hospitals. We were growing at a rate that would make many managers envious, but by standards of our own young industry, we were laggards.

In the mid-1970s, Bill Fickling changed the direction of Charter Medical Corporation. Charter Medical was the first major company in our industry to make a strategic decision that carried it off in a significantly different direction. At that time, Bill Fickling slashed overhead, tightened controls, and brought in new management. He also began to weed out the shopping centers and nursing homes that did not fit the future of the company. Most significantly, Fickling decided Charter Medical would become a leader in a relatively untapped sector of the investor-owned hospital industry—psychiatric care. There were several sound reasons for Charter Medical's new strategic thrust. First, there was an unmet need for psychiatric hospital beds. While virtually every medium-sized community has a good general hospital, several good-sized population centers in this country and throughout the world have no private free-standing psychiatric hospital. In fact, there are states that don't have a private free-standing psychiatric hospital.

In addition, new advances in drug treatment methods made it possible for patients to be treated effectively and safely in a comfortable, non-institutional environment. These new wonder drugs kept symptoms under control so patients could take part in many different therapies.

Before tranquilizers such as Thorazine and Stelazine, one-third of those suffering from acute schizophrenia, for example, were totally without hope. Another third could expect only slight improvement, with frequent recurrence of delusions and other symptoms that could make those patients a potential threat to themselves and others. Today, about nine out of ten patients experiencing first episodes of schizophrenia have the probability of excellent remission.

Depression, too, was formerly a disabling long-term illness. However, with the new generation of drugs, such as Elavil and Tofranil, many instances of depression can be treated effectively in a two- to three-week hospital stay. This is significant for our business, because depression is the most widespread mental illness in America, and one of the major reasons for admissions to psychiatric hospitals.

Another social trend that made this area of the business attractive to Charter Medical was the changing attitudes about mental illness. Not too many years ago, even going to a psychiatrist carried a tremendous stigma. That simply is not the case anymore.

The old snake pit stereotype has truly broken down. Indeed, many state mental institutions have released thousands of patients who formerly were no more than warehoused in giant hospitals. As sufferers have improved, mental illness has gradually been exposed to the lights of compassion and understanding.

We felt that the combination of existing market factors and emerging social trends presented a real opportunity for a quality-oriented company like Charter Medical to establish a reputation in an emerging medical specialty. We reasoned that, if we kept our focus on quality, we could obtain a position of industry leadership and all of the financial and other advantages that accrue to a leader.

What have been the results of our seizing that opportunity? At the beginning of 1976, Charter Medical owned and operated twelve hospitals. Today we have forty-four facilities open or under development in the United States and London, and a major health care services contract in Saudi Arabia. We have four new psychiatric hospitals opening in the next seven months. We expect to begin construction on at least six new facilities before the end of 1983. We have several major hospital-expansion programs under way and several regulatory applications pending to build new hospitals.

Since 1976, when we identified this strategy, revenues have grown at a compound annual rate of 27 percent. Our net income has compounded at 54 percent, earnings per share have compounded at 62 percent, and our return on equity has increased from 9 percent to more than 30 percent—and that's a compound rate of 22 percent.

This clearly is excellent growth, but what is going to happen through the rest of the 1980s?

With the continued increase in the average age of the population, the demand for quality health care is almost certain to increase also. Technology will continue to advance at a quantum rate. Much of that technology filters down very quickly to the health care industry. Developments like CAT scanners five years ago, nuclear magnetic resonance today, new drugs, new surgical techniques, bio-engineering—all these have a great effect on the capital required to be in this business, and on the entire health care industry.

There will be continuing pressure to control health care costs. I don't believe, however, that there will be any basic attack by government on the notion that health care is "free." We see that as the basic problem. Until patients feel they are at least a partner in paying the costs of services being rendered to them, there's going to be little control on costs.

The way medicine is practiced will continue to evolve in the 1980s. Physicians will continue to superspecialize. We will see more and more physicians coming together in groups. And we will see more and more alternative ways of practicing medicine.

For example, many physicians getting out of medical school today don't want to practice on a twenty-four-hour-per-day basis, with their leisure time and family life constantly subject to disruption by the relentless pocket beeper.

One alternative for these doctors is to practice in an immediate care center, such as those operated by Charter Medical. These centers are bridging the service gap between the traditional physician's office—which is available by appointment only, and only from 9 to 5—and the hospital emergency room—which typically is very expensive, and which can be very slow.

Immediate care centers, by contrast, are open eighteen hours a day or longer, and patients do not need an appointment. They are a cost-effective alternative delivery system that meets the needs and demands of our changing, more mobile society, and also satisfies the practice preferences of physicians who do not want to work more than forty hours a week. We are going to continue to see alternatives like immediate care centers.

We also will see continued growth for investor-owned health care groups such as Charter Medical. We will continue to see specialization in hospital care like that which our company embarked upon in the mid-1970s. Psychiatric hospital care is one form of specialization, and other forms are going to develop in this industry.

Although I've spent my entire professional life in the health care industry, I am still struck by the beautiful simplicity of helping to improve the quality of people's lives by investing private capital across a number of hospital facilities. There is no question in my mind that the management techniques introduced by the investor-owned industry will be deeply ingrained throughout even not-for-profit health care institutions by the turn of the century. This truly is a remarkable achievement. Let me draw on history for an example of how the health care industry traditionally has resisted innovation and change. Prior to 1865, more than half of all surgical patients died from complications following their operations. Then Sir Joseph Lister of Great Britain had the audacity to suggest that this incredible mortality rate might in some way be related to the fact that surgeons did not wash up before performing surgery. Lister was openly mocked and ridiculed.

Today it would be considered barbaric not to wash. But in those days, the surgeon was proud to leave the blood from his previous procedure on his hands and to wear the same surgical garb while he attended to the next patient. As Lister's views were grudgingly accepted over the following decade, the mortality rate from surgery dropped from approximately one in two to less than three in a hundred.

If it took 2,000 years for physicians to scrub up for surgery, then perhaps we should not be surprised that the application of sound business principles is something relatively new in the hospital industry. That's our major technology. Every other growth industry is talking about its technology. Our technology is just good management.

The success of the U.S. hospital management industry shows that, for organizations willing to take risks and to look at old problems in new ways, opportunities still exist to combine worthwhile public service with exceptional rewards. To people both inside and outside health care, that's perhaps the most important lesson to be learned from the success of the investor-owned hospital industry.

HOWARD R. KATZ

Construction: Changing Family Residences

Ocilla Industries is a manufacturer of mobile homes—the more popular current term is "manufactured housing"—with two factories in south Georgia. We produce about 5,000 homes per year and our homes are sold throughout the South from the East Coast as far west as New Mexico.

In early 1980, a number of factors combined to change the housing industry in the United States as we had known it for almost fifty years. While certain trends relating to the increased costs of home ownership had become evident before that time, it was still generally accepted that single-family detached home ownership was within the reach of middle-income Americans, and this type of home ownership was considered an essential part of the American dream. Yet economics were working against this dream.

At the end of 1979, the average selling price of a new site-built single family home, with an average of 1,700 square feet of living space, stood at approximately $72,000, up from almost $48,000 just three years earlier. With mortgage rates then at about 11 percent and an average down payment of 20 percent, this meant that the monthly payment on the old standard thirty-year mortgage was about $540 which, when added to property taxes and insurance, meant payments to the bank totaling about $650 a month.

In order to qualify for this mortgage, a potential homeowner needed an annual income in excess of $30,000 a year. This was still 50 percent more than the average household income of $20,000 a year. Home ownership, then, was still a realizable dream for the bulk of the middle class if they were willing to extend themselves just a little further in the amount of debt they assumed and to make some sacrifices in other areas of discretionary spending.

In early 1980, all that changed and probably forever. Mortgage rates jumped quickly to 17 percent and the selling price of the average home moved to $76,000. This meant a total monthly payment in excess of $1,000, requiring an income of $50,000 a year to qualify for the mortgage under the previous guidelines.

However, the cost of energy also was rising in an unprecedented manner and this added about $150 a month to consumer spending. Lenders were forced to reevaluate their guidelines and to place more stringent requirements on the potential homeowner's income necessary to qualify for a mortgage.

As if all this weren't enough, the potential home buyer faced yet another problem, the onset of a recession. That meant no longer relying on a continued rise in income or even continued employment.

As a result of all of these factors, the housing industry virtually collapsed in 1980, 1981, and 1982, with new construction at its lowest levels since World War II. For some calendar quarters, construction actually fell below the level of demolition, abandonment, and accidental destruction so you had a net decrease in the housing stock available for a growing population.

Housing starts fell from nearly two million units in 1978 to below one million units in 1982 and site-built homes with selling prices under $40,000 virtually disappeared from the market. Only 29,000 homes under $40,000 were sold in 1981 and probably even slightly fewer in 1982.

Manufactured or mobile home production, the primary source of housing under $40,000, also felt these increases in inflation and interest rates. Industry production fell from 275,000 units in 1978 to 220,000 units in 1980 but made a slight recovery to roughly 240,000 units in 1982.

Today, with mortgage rates lower and expected to continue their fall, the housing industry is expecting a significant upturn. Still, events of the past several years have made it unlikely that households with incomes below $50,000 will participate in this new buying activity.

The average price of a new site-built home is approximately $90,000, actually $91,600 for the month of January 1983. With mortgage rates at about 13½ percent as of March 1983, this yields the same monthly payment of $1,000 a month and serves to disqualify the large majority of Americans who do not already own a home.

What, then, are the choices for the average American family? Some of the gap between the cost to construct housing and what the consumer can afford will be bridged by other types of conventionally built housing. These include condominiums, townhouses, duplexes, and garden apartments, and these alternatives already have proven themselves to be both acceptable and desirable to a large number of families.

It's also likely that conventionally built detached housing will continue to be down-sized to the 800 square foot to 1,200 square foot range as a method of making the home more affordable by bringing it down into that $50,000 range. Recent subdivisions of these smaller homes in the western Sunbelt markets have sold extremely well as builders scramble to get more lots out of their available land positions and to build a house that buyers can qualify for.

However, these alternatives still do not offer a realistic opportunity for home ownership to a large group of families with annual income levels in the $10,000 to $25,000 range. We believe that this group increasingly will turn to manufactured housing in one form or another to meet their needs.

A "manufactured home" refers to a home built in a factory using production assembly line techniques. Manufactured homes are further broken down into mobile, modular, panelized, prefabricated, and a variety of other terms.

Mobile homes are built to a national standard developed by the Department of Housing and Urban Development (HUD) and leave the factory as completed units on their own wheels. Once at the site, the wheels are removed and the house is installed on a concrete foundation and hooked up to existing plumbing and electrical supplies. Mobile homes range in size from as small as 500 square feet up to as large as 2,200 square feet. The manufacturers of these homes sell them primarily to independent retailers, who then resell them to the consumers.

Modular homes also leave the factory complete, but are built to state or regional building codes and usually are accepted for zoning purposes on the same basis as a conventionally built house. Panelized prefabricated homes and other variations are generally shipped in sections and then assembled at the site.

Of all of these types of manufactured homes, the mobile home is currently the most popular, accounting for approximately $5 billion in annual retail sales. About eight and a half million Americans now live in the existing four million mobile homes. They have proven to be particularly popular with young, newlywed buyers and with retirees. There are many reasons, aside from the underlying economic factors described earlier, for this popularity and our belief is that manufactured housing will continue to gain acceptance in market share.

First, since 1976 all manufactured homes have been built to a national standard established by HUD. These standards regulate the design and construction of the home, the structural considerations, and the performance of the heating, electrical, and plumbing systems. A HUD seal is affixed to the house, which lets the consumer know that it has been built to HUD standards.

Second, because of these standards, the home is usually very energy efficient, which leads to further savings in the way of energy usage.

Third, there has been a dramatic improvement in the appearance of manufactured homes. The industry and its suppliers have come a long way from the trailer image of the early 1950s, and homes are now built with an extensive choice of exterior and interior materials and design. Virtually all of the features available for site-built housing are now available in a manufactured home.

Fourth, along with the improvements in the house itself have come improvements in site selection and community layout. Mobile home communities are, in some cases, virtually indistinguishable from site-built developments.

Fifth, along with improved appearance, zoning restrictions against mobile homes have become far less prevalent. The state of New Jersey has gone so far as to require each community in New Jersey to set aside land for mobile home use.

Sixth, all of these factors have led to longer term financing from banking institutions and have opened up the FHA and VA programs for manufactured homes. For a mobile home permanently sited on a buyer's own land, mortgage terms are comparable to terms for a site-built home.

However, the primary reason for the growing popularity of manufactured housing is its low cost relative to conventional site-built housing. In 1981, the average selling price for all types of manufactured homes was $19 per square foot. This is roughly half the average for site-built housing of $39 per square foot.

While some of this significant price advantage comes from the use of different materials, there are some inherent economic advantages in building housing on a factory production lot.

They include lower labor costs resulting from standard designs and specific task assignments and not having labor hampered by any form of inclement weather, because employees are working indoors. There are some significant purchasing advantages because of the sheer volume of materials delivered to the same place, the factory, on a regular basis. For example, during the next year we will buy 6,000 refrigerators and 6,000 stoves. Mobile home manufacturers generally receive the most favorable pricing treatment from appliance manufacturers.

Finally, mobile home producers have lower capital requirements because we have a very short production cycle, typically only two to three weeks. Inventories can be turned as many as twenty-five times a year and our accounts receivable are typically less than thirty days because the industry structure allows retailers to floorplan the home with finance companies. All of these factors result in a lower cost of doing business which is translated into lower costs for the consumer.

Before I describe how Ocilla has responded to these activities and problems in the housing industry, I would like to put the preceding comments about mobile homes into perspective. While they have come a long way and will continue to improve, they are certainly not for everyone. There are many reasons why people choose the type of home they would like to live in, and cost is only one of those factors. Mobile homes are primarily a way of delivering affordable housing to a segment of the population that simply cannot afford conventionally built homes.

What has Ocilla done about all of this? In early 1980, we all had the same problems. We were what was defined as a medium-priced producer of mobile homes with retail prices in the $15,000 to $22,000 range.

While demand for our products remained strong, with mortgage rates at 17 to 20 percent our buyers could no longer qualify for mortgages. Within thirty days, we formulated a plan to deal with this problem that capitalized on our strengths and had some very simple objectives. Our first objective was to maximize our potential for growth. Second, we wanted to reduce the impact of interest rates on our business. We were absolutely shocked, along with everyone else, that interest rates could move as much as eight points in as little as eight months and we anticipated that the volatility of interest rates could be a continuing problem. We further felt that there was no realistic chance for an orderly growth progression, if we allowed ourselves to be dependent upon low interest rates.

The strategy we chose was to manufacture and sell the lowest priced homes we could without sacrificing our reputation for quality and reliability. Within sixty days, we were manufacturing homes with retail prices far below $10,000 and, in some cases, as low as $7,000. This meant that any potential buyer who earned as little as $250 a week and had a good credit rating could qualify. It further meant that if you could qualify to purchase any home built in this country, you could qualify to buy our homes—which typically are 800 to 900 square feet but can go up to 1,400 square feet.

In the three years since we began this program, the results have been absolutely astonishing. We have gone from $9 million in sales to $30 million in the year ended February 1983 and we anticipate volume in the $40 million to $50 million range next year. Our earnings have quadrupled from slightly below $400,000 to somewhere in the area of $1.5 million. We are looking for significant improvement next year. We now produce as many as twenty-five homes a day instead of the four middle-priced homes we were producing when we converted to this program.

Our manufacturing capacity has quadrupled in response to an order backlog that has been as high as five months, a situation unheard of in an industry that usually works on two- to three-week backlogs. Three years ago, we had seventy-five dealers. Today we have 350, and we'll attempt to reach as many as 500 dealers in the next year. The number of employees has quadrupled to over 400 and all of this was accomplished during the three worst housing years in the past forty years.

Growth was very important to us, and we simply refused not to grow.

Let's look at some of the rewards for growth and our performance. Ocilla is now a publicly held company with 500 shareholders and a market valuation in excess of $40 million from an initial equity investment of $1 million three years ago. Two public offerings have raised $9½ million in equity capital for the company and our balance sheet shows $14 million in cash out of total assets of $19 million. Our long-term debt consists of one industrial revenue bond totaling $1 million. Growth has allowed us to hire the best possible people and thereby make us even more competitive for the future. We have been able to capitalize our company permanently with enough equity to support $100 million in sales. We can also anticipate that we will achieve additional growth from the commanding position we have now in our segment of the marketplace.

Why were we able to grow during such a difficult period? Basically because we decided to satisfy a market that no one else really wanted to satisfy. It's really much easier to make $5,000 by selling a $30,000 house than it is to make a lot of $600 profits by selling a lot of $7,000 houses. What allowed us to do it was management and the efforts of our operating people led by an extraordinary manager, Lige Waldron, who is in south Georgia today producing twenty-five houses. We were able to begin to produce lower priced units in a very short time because he and his staff selected the materials and developed the necessary production techniques and efficiencies that allowed us our growth and success.

One of the questions asked about growth is: Does geography help? It certainly helped us to be in the expanding Sunbelt markets, but the real benefit for this half-transplanted New Yorker has been the opportunity to deal with the friendly and helpful people that I've met in the Southeast in the past three years and for that I want to thank you all.

DONALD L. KOCH

Changing the Corporate Culture through Information Systems

American society is moving out of the age of industrialization and into the age of information. In the industrial age, standardization, centralization, synchronization, uniformity, and mass production permeated our entire society. But today, new technologies, new forms of energy, new modes of thinking have spawned a civilization of diverse attitudes, knowledge, and beliefs—a society that is breaking through the constraints of the industrial environment. In *The Third Wave*, Alvin Toffler depicts the new society as a diverse, fragmented culture dependent upon information and communications to hold it together:

For the more diverse the civilization—the more differentiated its technology, energy forms and people—the more information must flow between its constituent parts if the entirety is to hold together, particularly under the stress of high change. . . . The more uniform we are, the less we need to know about each other in order to predict one another's behavior. As people around us grow more individualized or de-massified, we need more information—signals and cues—to predict, even roughly, how they are going to behave toward us. And unless we can make such forecasts we cannot work or even live together.

As a result, people and organizations continually crave more information and the entire system begins to pulse with higher and higher flows of data. By forcing up the amount of information needed for the social system to cohere, and the speeds at which it must be exchanged, the Third Wave shatters the framework of the obsolete, overloaded Second Wave info-sphere and constructs a new one to take its place.[1]

For the most part, corporations today still operate in an environment based on the concepts of the industrial society. Few corporations have found successful techniques for migrating to the more fluid forms of management required in a rapidly changing environment. Yet enlightened executives acknowledge the changes occurring in society and recognize the necessity of joining the information age to retain their competitive advantage.

We will attempt to explain how corporate management can change an organization's culture using computer information systems. We'll include a step-by-step discussion of our experience at the Federal Reserve Bank of Atlanta Research Department in increasing the productivity of office workers. While computer technology can play a large role in eliminating routine mindless tasks, we found that it is only part of a greater management effort to leverage one's mind and increase human potential.

ORGANIZATIONAL CHANGE

To prepare the corporation to operate effectively in the information age, executive management must first identify the organization's current culture. In many cases, management techniques that have proved successful in the manufacturing environment are being adopted in office settings. This management style places a heavy emphasis on procedures, standardization, automating mechanical processes, and scheduling. Management rewards workers who are obedient, punctual, and willing to perform rote tasks. In an "industrial culture," office automation tends to imitate factory automation by mechanizing existing functions. This mechanistic environment of the industrial age, however, inhibits the information worker, who must be a creative and active thinker. Great strides in office productivity will occur only when the organization is unleashed from the restrictions of the industrial environment.

Productivity in the industrial age was measured in terms of quantity. The objective was to satisfy a growing population's appetite for more and more consumer goods. But the mechanization process reached diminishing returns when standardization and mass production became resistant to change. The standard example is the U.S. automobile industry, once the showcase of American productivity and successful management techniques. The "machine" became so big, inflexible, and resistant to change that it threatened to destroy itself.

Productivity in the information age involves creative thinking, flexibility, and the ability to change and adapt quickly. Information workers must rely less on vertical, sequential, logical, left-brained thinking. The new environment requires that people break away from old patterns of thought.

In his book on lateral thinking, Edward de Bono offers a method of finding creative solutions to problems—a technique that can be learned. The commonly used thought process, logical and methodical, uses patterns to handle information. It processes new information in relation to an already established pattern in the mind. According to de Bono,

The mind . . . allows information to organize itself into patterns. This self-organizing, self-maximizing, memory system is very good at creating patterns and that is the effectiveness of the mind. But inseparable from the great usefulness of a patterning system are certain limitations. In such a system it is easy to combine patterns or to add to them, but it is extremely difficult to restructure them, for the patterns control the attention. . . . Creativity involves restructuring (of patterns) with emphasis on the escape from restricting patterns. Lateral thinking involves restructuring, escape and the provocation of new patterns. . . . It is concerned with breaking out of the concept prisons of old ideas. This leads to change in attitude and approach; to looking in a different way at things which have always been looked at in the same ways. Liberation from old ideas and the stimulation of new ones are twin aspects of lateral thinking.[2]

If productivity is to be stimulated by creative thought, the working environment must provide the proper atmosphere, resources, incentives, and rewards to promote this new kind of productivity.

APPROPRIATE MANAGEMENT STYLE

The foundation for managing knowledge workers rests on a clearly defined management style. Traditional techniques successful in controlling manufacturing processes fail to motivate knowledge workers. We found the approach that works best is "collegiality." Decisions should involve open debate among all players, because decisions arrived at through open dialogue are more likely to be based on sound judgment.

At the foundation of the decision-making process lies "dynamic tension." This concept implies a positive and constructive friction between employee and employer to ensure that the best possible decisions are made on a case-by-case basis. Freedom of expression is encouraged under this system as long as that freedom is handled with concern for professional objectivity and respect.

Unlike the traditional hierarchical management, the collegial approach often works from the bottom up. The real "high priest" of the decision-making link is the person who is most effective and who makes decisions that stand the test of time in contributing to products, regardless of his or her position on the organization chart. In such an open environment, petty persuasions or propositions that lack proper scrutiny can be rejected quickly. Open debate, bottom-up decision making, internal consistency, and appreciation for all employees' strengths are the benchmarks of an effective management process.

The attributes of effective management frequently are hard to find in a large organization where adherence to standard procedures is often more highly rewarded than high-quality, high-quantity production. In the corporate world, firms often motivate employees by encouraging them to acquire shares of stock in their companies. In another sense, employees maximize their "human equity" by performing well. They buy "shares of time" in their own lives through their work. They can enhance the quality of their life by making a real contribution, or they can perform in a mediocre way, which devalues the institution and their own human equity. The best knowledge workers will seek out environments that challenge their potential and allow them to "maximize their equity" through growth, experimentation, and hard work.

To create this environment, a management system must offer both accountability and autonomy. Employees must be able to make autonomous decisions and implement actions freely without regard to what their superiors think, as long as the controls of accountability and responsibility are in place. Along with enjoying the freedom to act, the decision maker accepts responsibility if such decisions fail to produce tangible results. With this system, innovation and creativity are rewarded and employees make their decisions based on what is best for the organization rather than what might satisfy the boss.

In such a system, success and failure are easily recognized. Annually, each employee establishes a performance contract that is reviewed several times a year. Success comes when one is able to fulfill the contract. High achievers prosper but, in such an environment, some individuals who fail to perform recognize they would do better elsewhere.

FEDERAL RESERVE BANK OF ATLANTA RESEARCH DEPARTMENT

This was the new style of management introduced early in 1981 to the Federal Reserve Bank of Atlanta Research Department, the research arm of the central bank that serves a six-state southeastern district. Today the Research Department is segmented into eight teams, generally consisting of three economists, three research analysts, two clerical support staff, and two student interns. Research content focuses on four major themes:

National Economic Policy. The central mission of the Federal Reserve is monetary policy. Each Reserve Bank president shares a seat on the Federal Open Market Committee, the Federal Reserve body that oversees monetary policy, and requires independent staff work from his or her research department.

The Southeast. The Southeast District is a high-growth region, undergoing high rates of in-migration and requiring importation of capital. Regional information about the Southeast is in high demand and short supply. Analysis of such a region can be important to national policy makers as well as to institutions in the region.

Financial Services Deregulation. The pace of financial innovation and deregulation makes this a research area with great potential, particularly when oriented toward the future rather than the past. Competition in the southeastern market for financial services offers important opportunities for research on the entire deregulating financial system.

Payments Research. The Atlanta Fed processes a high proportion of the checks handled by the Federal Reserve System. Atlanta pioneered in electronic funds transfer. The Bank has one of the most efficient operations areas in the system and is committed to remaining in the forefront of operations excellence. Therefore, Research focuses on the future of the payments system and the Fed's role in it.

Our research teams are decentralized and exercise unusual freedom to develop products within agreed overall goals. This is far from a laissez-faire proposition, however. Research manuscripts, for instance, must be relevant, literate, and oriented toward the future. Team leaders work under performance agreements, which they draft themselves and negotiate with department management.

The department is extraordinarily results-oriented. As measured by printed material delivered to our market, productivity increased 920 percent from late 1980 to early 1983. Our flagship product, the *Economic Review,* was expanded from a bimonthly to a monthly publication in 1981 and doubled in number of pages per issue. Circulation of that magazine, which carries economic and financial articles, increased from 17,800 in 1980 to 30,500 by early 1983. A newer semimonthly newsletter, *Insight,* currently reaches 6,000 subscribers. The department has sponsored three major conferences in two years, each attracting an average of 300 top-level executives. Proceedings from each conference were edited and published in book form. Additionally, department economists prepare a 100-page briefing booklet every six weeks to support the Bank's president at meetings of the Federal Open Market Committee. In addition, a regional economic data base containing over 2,000 statistical series and updated monthly by the department soon will be offered to the public via an electronic information system.

The new level of output came from the same basic group of people who worked in Research prior to the management change. There has been a net increase in staff of only one full-time person since January 1981. Of the eight team leaders, five worked at the Atlanta Fed under the old style of management. Only three of fourteen professionals chose to leave when the management philosophy changed.

Our eight team leaders are encouraged to use their ingenuity, technology, and networks of outside contacts to develop products. They work with visiting scholars, college interns, part-time specialists, and the department's facilities for microcomputer data bases, information retrieval, and publications production. The effective use of computer technology is only part of the reason for the increased productivity. Without the appropriate culture, as I have described, the technology could hardly have generated these gains.

USING TECHNOLOGY TO LEVERAGE THE MIND

Knowledge work can be defined as any job that requires gathering information; analyzing, reshaping, integrating, transforming information into decisions and recommendations; and generating information output in printed or spoken form. This description fits a multitude of jobs in our society: lawyers, doctors, managers, accountants, ministers, secretaries, engineers, investors, computer programmers, salespeople, corporate executives, financial analysts, strategic planners, regulators, bankers, economists, scientists, marketing specialists, purchasing agents, and educators. The tools these people use to accomplish their jobs are generally limited to pencil, paper, telephone, and calculator. Yet the technology available today can free knowledge workers from routine, mindless tasks and allows them to utilize more of their potential. This was accomplished at the Federal Reserve Bank of Atlanta Research Department through a process applicable to any knowledge-work environment.

From the first, Research management focused on automating department functions that would provide the most leverage in meeting the overall department objective: elevating the organization to a center of excellence for economic understanding in the Southeast. Automation helped to meet that objective by providing the means to increase quantity of output (more printed pages), shorten the lead time required to produce output or respond to requests, and improve the quality, relevance, and timeliness of output. Management recognized several principles very early which guided the decision process in choosing equipment to meet these needs.

1. Technology must be applications driven. We know it is essential to keep up with new technologies and monitor the direction of the industry, but we attempt to introduce only proven technologies and well-tested equipment. For example, "bubble memory" at one point was lauded as the wave of the future for storage media. We tried two portable terminals that had bubble memory, but made no major investment. The technology never delivered the results it promised. Weight proved to be a problem and the commands to exercise the memory were cumbersome. Today, CMOS technology is beginning to be used in consumer electronic products as an information storage device.

Although the products are very new, the technology—which permits more transistors to be compressed on a semiconductor chip—is at least ten years old. We are likely to be a major purchaser of new portable computers using CMOS chips because the technology's usefulness has been proven.

2. Vendor competition is better than vendor standardization. By introducing several vendors into the organization, each must continuously bid against others. This tends to "keep the vendor honest" and to maximize discounts. Additionally, when an organization becomes totally entrenched with one vendor's products, it becomes extremely difficult to change.

3. The vendor should be scrutinized meticulously for financial viability, innovative spirit, commitment to the product line, and manufacturing quality. This scrutiny is essential whether an organization is buying one or one thousand units. We personally visit the headquarters of each company selected as a vendor and talk extensively with management as if we were planning to invest in the firm's stock. Essentially, we are making a substantial investment in each firm we do business with, and we want to be sure that our investment is being well managed.

4. The decision to purchase a certain type of equipment must stand the test of time. We want to be able to look back in three years and say, "That was a good decision." For us to be able to say that, the company must still be active in the industry and its product must have been accepted within our organization, must have met our growing needs, and must still be usable.

5. Equipment should be designed to meet a specific need yet should be flexible enough to expand with growing needs. A piece of equipment cannot be all things to all people. A commercial word processor should be used almost exclusively for preparing final drafts of reports. But the author can input first drafts directly on less expensive equipment. If the word processing equipment includes communications capability, the early drafts can be transmitted to it from any machine in any location for final preparation.

6. All computer equipment should have such a capability so that work done on one system can be transmitted to another. This capability allows text to be keyed once and only once. Documents can be passed from personal computer to word processor to phototypesetter. We have found simple asynchronous RS232 communications at speeds of 30 or 120 characters per second quite adequate in this capacity.

With these six principles in mind, the Research Department began a systematic acquisitions program in early 1981. Four major types of equipment were chosen to facilitate our work: dedicated word processing equipment, desk-top graphics computers, personal computers, and portable computers. We have accumulated enough equipment to provide a computer for every full-time staff member.

WORD PROCESSING

The Research Department's output is virtually always in the form of printed material or, more graphically expressed, "black ink on white paper." Therefore, we had to improve the means of generating our publications.

Before the automation effort began in 1981, the entire department was funneling work to a word processing pool consisting of two work stations, two operators, a supervisor, and a proofreader. Almost all typing was done by the word processing pool. This arrangement was a source of frustration for many economists and research analysts who found themselves waiting for days to have their work processed.

Our first automation effort was to dismantle the typing pool and distribute secretarial and word processing support directly to each team. In this way, a team responsible for a given level of output could control all its resources. The excuse that a project was held up in the typing pool was no longer valid. A secretary was matched to each team by allowing each to choose the team to work on. In every case, secretaries were given their first or second choice of teams. The department leased enough word processing equipment (seven stations with Cathode-ray tube terminals, or CRTs) to give each secretary a station plus extra one-line display keyboards to tie into the system. Economists' and analysts' offices and cubicles were wired for word processors with one-line display keyboards. In this way, five extra keyboards acquired at lower cost than the work stations were shared among professionals within their own work spaces. Professionals began inputting their own reports and memos to speed up the production process, the first step toward eliminating the "legal pad draft."

The results of this one effort were outstanding. Secretaries spent less time typing and retyping from handwritten manuscripts. But the secretaries' jobs weren't threatened. Their time shifted to other responsibilities on the teams, which gave them a greater sense of ownership in the department. Where word processor operators in the past had been required only to key in material, as secretaries they now had to proof and correct for grammar. They were given more diverse responsibilities such as planning meetings, setting up files, updating data bases, and controlling requisitions. As more and more professionals became interested in doing their own word processing, the secretaries proved invaluable as teachers. Roles were reversed as the professional began to depend on the secretary to teach him or her a new skill. Professionals who had proclaimed "I don't type" soon found it much easier to keyboard ideas rather than to write them out.

The professionals' increased use of the keyboard allowed a tremendous increase in speed and output without increasing staff. Generally, a professional keys ideas into the word processor in rough form. Then he or she works with the team secretary to edit the document into final form. The real time savings comes from reducing duplication of effort when the ideas initially go down in machine-readable format. As more professionals demanded full capability, we added word processing stations. Since the initial twelve word processing work stations were introduced in early 1981, the number has doubled.

Within months of introducing the word processors, we found that the increased output facilitated by the word processors was creating a bottleneck at the final production stage. Most of our final output is typeset for publication, and we were still sending manuscripts out to a commercial typesetter to re-key. The process, costly and time consuming, was inhibiting our stepped-up printing schedule. We purchased a phototypesetter for $22,000 to be operated in-house by our own employees. It paid for itself in four months. The process now is for the author and secretary to create a manuscript on the word processor, then pass the diskette to a staff editor whose revisions are keyed into the document. When all final editing is complete, the document is transmitted to the phototypesetter and typesetting formats are applied. A graphics staff then lays out the publication and sends it to the bank's print shop or to a commercial printer.

This is one example of the importance of flexibility in equipment. We knew we needed communications capability in our word processors, but we did not know that we would be buying a typesetter. The flexibility of our equipment allowed us to bring in the typesetter, connect it to the word processor, and begin operations quickly. It is also important to note that the word processor and the typesetter are supplied by two distinct vendors. A company that specializes in office automation tools supplies our word processors. A vendor whose specialty is optics makes the phototypesetting equipment. Each vendor is good at what it does. We consider it unlikely that the same vendor could offer both the best of word processing technology and the best of phototypesetting technology.

In each installation of new equipment, we tended to underestimate the demand. We anticipated that the typesetter would be utilized only twenty hours a week. However, the demand has been so great that we now have a full-time operator and a part-time operator who works after normal hours. Additionally, another employee has been trained to operate the typesetter and can fill in during peak demand. The machine is used about twelve hours every weekday and frequently on weekends. This word processor-phototypesetter combination has streamlined our production process tremendously and continues to support the production of printed material.

DESK-TOP GRAPHICS COMPUTERS

The Research Department monitors and analyzes a large group of economic time series such as unemployment, gross national product, housing starts, and interest rates. A particular data series may be used as frequently as daily or weekly or it may be needed only on an ad hoc basis for special studies or to fill special requests.

This need for various time series is not unique to economic data. Internal data monitoring for management purposes has the same character. Anyone who analyzes trends for decision or research purposes needs data bases that represent aggregates over time. Yet computer storage of corporate data traditionally has been structured for accounting purposes. The accounting data bases focus on only one point in time and are very detailed.

Recognizing this need, we acquired four desk-top graphics terminals, later expanded to seven, with hard disk storage. We developed data bases to fill our needs by transferring existing data from mainframe computers and keying in data received in printed form. We wrote several simple programs that allowed for updating the data, displaying the data in list or graphic form, and doing simple analysis. A three-member team is constantly building, updating, and documenting the data bases. The entire department has access to the data through user-friendly menu-driven programs. The graphics computers are mounted on mobile carts that anyone can move into an office or cubicle. Having economic data immediately accessible in graphic form has enhanced the quality of analysis and shortened the time required to do lengthy studies or to respond to special requests.

Of course, the data bases and software cannot accomplish everything we need. An economist or analyst must directly input certain data series, not regularly maintained, to perform graphics analysis. Also, users sometimes want to conduct more sophisticated analysis than our software can handle. In those cases, he or she can transfer the data from our graphics terminals to a mainframe computer and use econometric modeling packages for the analysis. Then the user can download the results for graphic display. The capabilities that are missing represent only about 20 percent of our work. The 80 percent that has been automated effectively using local computer intelligence has greatly increased our capabilities to provide timely analysis.

While graphics analysis can be performed on a regular personal computer, we found our demand for graphics so great that it warranted a computer designed specifically for that function by a company specializing in graphics. We chose a flexible system that is programmable and has asynchronous RS232 communications. Peripherals tie into the equipment easily. As the data bases grew rapidly, we invested in a 32-megabyte hard disk for central data storage. To insure the data integrity, we centralized the job of maintaining these internal data bases within the department.

PERSONAL COMPUTERS

One year after we began our automation effort we found that, while a few people were becoming expert with the computer, others shied away from it. The graphics computers still required custom programming and had to be used for specific predefined functions. We saw the need for a personal productivity tool that professionals could use creatively to increase their effectiveness. We acquired three personal computers with standard text editing, spreadsheet, communications, and data base management programs. The demand for these machines quickly proved far greater than the supply. Professionals found them to be a tool they could use not only to write reports and display data graphically, but also to do large calculations, build simple econometric models, and organize data. The spreadsheet capability alone gave them the flexibility to do more and better analysis.

We encouraged employees to take the machines home over weekends to gain familiarity with them. Most learned by reading a manual and experimenting. Others waited until a colleague who had gained some knowledge could show them how to get started. We borrowed some game packages from the local computer vendor for our people to use in off hours. Playing games reduced the fear factor and increased the intimacy between human and machine.

A few months later we purchased five more personal computers, then another four more-sophisticated units. Complaints continued to come in—"I could do so much with this machine if I knew I could get my hands on it when I need it." Our latest round of purchases added ten more personal computers, boosting the inventory to twenty-two. With those units we were able to assign computers to individuals rather than requiring users to share. This arrangement works much better because now the machine truly is a *personal* productivity tool.

The personal computers are used much more for word processing than we expected. Professionals and analysts take them home to write reports free from office interruptions, then transmit the document by modem to a word processor for final formatting and editing. With the personal computer, to-do lists are kept on computers rather than on note pads. Data base management programs are becoming more and more useful for tracking projects, organizing information collected for a project, and analyzing survey or questionnaire results. The personal computers are being tied into a local area network to enhance data sharing and to develop an electronic communications scheme.

Initially, some problems occurred with servicing the personal computers, since most vendors require users to bring the system to the outlet for repair. We initiated an on-site service contract with our vendor that works well. Also, we thought it outrageous to purchase a separate software package for every machine, but found that the problems involved in sharing software outweigh the dollar outlay. Researchers have standard packages available at all times. We have a central check-out station for other packages that are used infrequently.

PORTABLE TERMINALS AND COMPUTERS

Initially we invested in portable terminals for employees who were involved exclusively in time-sharing work. We kept that investment small—four portable terminals. We also wanted to develop a system so those who travel could communicate with the office. We developed a system in which the traveler signed on to a time-sharing vendor and typed a message into a file stored on the vendor's disk. The traveler's secretary could sign on to the same account and retrieve the file. The secretary would prepare messages on a word processor and then, once or twice a day, sign on to the time-sharing vendor and transfer the messages to a file for the traveler to read.

The original system worked fine, but the fifteen-pound terminal proved too bulky to carry on short trips. Now we have a three-pound portable computer that allows the traveler to prepare messages off line and then upload them to the host computer. Also, the traveler can retrieve the secretary's messages, edit a letter off line, and then send it back. The training required to do this is minimal. We now use more sophisticated electronic mail offered by the time-sharing vendor. It allows for greater privacy in sending files and verifying that messages have been read, and makes the system easier for several people to use in concert. In this way a person can always be in touch with the office and can respond to messages and correspondence that come in while he or she is away. Many tasks can be completed remotely that may have been delayed for days without this system.

USER ACCEPTANCE

User acceptance is often considered a potential problem in introducing new technology in the work environment. We found, without exception, that once a person is exposed to the benefits of the machine for a particular job, he or she is hooked.

When we first introduced word processing, for instance, a veteran secretary adamantly opposed using the system. We sent her to a training class anyway. For months she fussed whenever something went wrong with the machine—but she did learn to use it. The true test came when she transferred to another department within a year after being introduced to word processing. She said she would take the other job *only if she could take her word processing equipment with her!* We knew then that once anyone learns a new skill, he or she can never go back to less efficient operations.

SUMMARY

Transforming an organization so it can operate effectively in the information age requires that people shed industrial age values and adopt new approaches and incentives. Whereas the old environment valued standardization, procedures, and machines, the new organization thrives on creativity, individuality, and flexibility. Industrial "road blocks" should be recognized and moved to provide the proper environment for the information age worker.

The major contrasts between the old and the new office environments are:

1. People—not machines—are central to productivity.
2. Power today is in the hands of those who possess information and can turn it into knowledge; the old hierarchical system is less important in our new era.
3. Emphasis is on results—not rigid adherence to standards.
4. Technology is seen as liberating people's minds to improve productivity—not as enslaving them to their own inventions.

The computer—introduced during the height of the industrial age—was regarded like any other piece of machinery; it mass-produced numbers instead of widgets. The equipment's expense made large, centralized mainframes the most efficient approach. Today, computer components are so inexpensive that it is becoming much more efficient to distribute the computing power to users. To accomplish that task, we must change people's perspective on using computers. To raise productivity to a higher plateau in the age of information, we must find ways to develop the mind, promote creative thinking, and facilitate the rapid exchange of information and ideas. The computer, utilized efficiently in a receptive information-age environment, holds the key to that increased productivity. The technology is available now for business to begin making tremendous productivity gains. To survive in a competitive world, corporate America cannot afford to wait.

NOTES

I would like to thank Delores Steinhauser of the Atlanta Fed Research Department staff for her valuable contributions to this presentation.

1. Alvin Toffler, *The Third Wave* (New York: William Morrow & Co., 1980), p. 183.

2. Edward de Bono, *Lateral Thinking: Creativity Step by Step* (New York: Harper & Row, 1970), pp. 10–11.

III. EMERGING GROWTH INDUSTRIES

Donald L. Koch, Moderator

Let's now turn to the subject of emerging growth industries.

We've looked at management excellence earlier, and I'm sure we can expect further observations on the subject. Superior management is widely recognized as one of the vital factors in the success of any company. In this panel, several CEOs will detail their management experiences in emerging growth industries. Unlike executives who direct traditional companies, the chairmen and presidents of today's new high-technology firms cannot continue simply steering the same course as their predecessors. They are, in effect, corporate pioneers, carving out new directions and new technologies.

First in line will be John T. Hartley, Jr., president and CEO of the Harris Corporation of Melbourne, Florida, a manufacturer of high-technology communication and information processing equipment, discussing electronics—which he describes as part of the wave of the future.

He'll be followed by J. Leland Strange, a cofounder of the Quadram Corporation, a Norcross, Georgia, firm that specializes in microcomputer enhancement products. He'll discuss minicomputers and telecommunications.

Finally, we will have James L. Bast, president of the Dictaphone Corporation, to examine the prospects for future rapid growth in automated office equipment.

JOHN T. HARTLEY, JR.

Electronics: High Technology Is the Wave of the Future

Harris is a technology based company. Our fundamental strategy is the innovative application of advanced technology to give our products, hopefully, a competitive lead in the market niches we try to serve. We do not try to be all things to all people in electronics. There are certain areas in electronics in which we have chosen not to participate, consumer electronics being one of them.

On the other hand, we have selected market segments or niches in electronics and communications technology and we tend to focus and specialize on those areas.

There have been dramatic changes taking place in our domestic and, in fact, our world economies. In the last fifty years or so, we have gone from an agricultural society to an industrial society. Now, Daniel Bell would argue that we are in the postindustrial era, in which the service industries will dominate and continue to dominate. But while I would agree with that observation, I think it has been made possible—and will continue to be made possible—by the success our industrial-based companies, in particular high-technology companies, have had in providing the tools for our service industry.

Now, I think electronics is at the forefront of that. I think that certainly what is happening in industries such as banking and retail are being made possible by the advances in electronics. I am going to cover some of the underlying technologies we believe are indicators of where those applications, those products, those markets are heading. As an integral part of our strategy, we tend to follow very closely what is happening in the technology areas and then try to apply those technologies to our products in an innovative way.

Let me single out a few of the technologies we believe to be the most significant in terms of determining where we are headed in the 1980s and on into the 1990s.

There are six technologies that I intend to discuss briefly. There is no significance in the ranking order with the exception of the first. Many people have asked me over the years to indicate to them, in a company like Harris, what are the things that we ought to watch in order to tell what will be happening in the future. My advice to those people has been and continues to be to watch what is happening in the semiconductor area. That is at the leading edge of everything going on in the electronics business; it's the hydrocarbon fuel of the electronics business, the basic building block of the business.

And many of the great products that you've heard about are really dependent on the progress that has been made in the area of semiconductors. So the subject of VLSI circuits as they relate to semiconductor technology is very important.

I think it is well understood by most people that very large scale integrated circuits have made possible a number of the rapid advances in computers and a number of other products. This is taking place because of the density that we have been able to incorporate in a single integrated circuit. Since the 1960s, when the very first integrated circuit was developed, we have tended to approximately double the number of components on a circuit each year.

We are now placing one million components on an integrated circuit and producing these in quantity, supplying them to the people who can build them into innovative products that meet the needs of the current and future society. This very rapid rate of change that is taking place in the density of these circuits and the functions that can be incorporated in them is a fundamental underpinning of the electronics business.

One microprocessor circuit being developed at Harris, which will be introduced in the spring, is referred to as a CMOS circuit. It is a complementary metal oxide semiconductor circuit. It is a version of INTEL's very popular microprocessor, the 8086 and CMOS. The 8086 holds over 50 percent of the microprocessor marketplace presently.

We can get on one circuit, which is approximately a quarter inch on a side, computing power that exceeds the IBM 360/50 series computer in terms of instructions executed. That 1960s computer was some hundred cubic feet in size, while this is a quarter inch in size. The cost of the system at that time was around $750,000 to $1 million. This circuit will sell for somewhere in the $40–$50 range.

In less than twenty years we have seen that kind of change take place. "Dramatic" to me seems to be an understatement, and I live in this business. I think that even our most sophisticated managers fail to understand the implications of what is really happening in this area of semiconductor technology. And I think that if the progress is extrapolated into the late 1980s and the 1990s it is going to give great opportunity to our overall electronic businesses and the application of these products into new products.

The advantages of CMOS technology include the fact that it uses much less power. One problem being encountered by putting more and more components on a very small space is that each component tends to generate some heat. When you put a million elements on a very small space, the heating introduced finally reaches a point where the circuit will no longer function. Since CMOS technology allows very low power, you can therefore get higher density of packaging and full temperature range operation. These circuits will operate in boiling water or well below freezing and they have a high immunity to electrical interference. They are opening up a number of new applications for us.

The introduction of something called gate-array technology is going to be a driving force in the future. Gate arrays allow users of integrated circuits to come to manufacturers and very quickly, in a matter of weeks, have custom-integrated circuits designed and manufactured for their unique applications. So we're seeing very rapid advances taking place in this area.

All of the examples I have mentioned have been based upon silicon. Silicon is a commonly available material. It is sand or quartz, basically, prepared in a very special way. But there are limitations as to what can be done with silicon technology. A few of us have been working to apply other materials to the semiconductor area to achieve improved performance.

Some circuits are being built of a material called gallium arsenide. Gallium arsenide has been around for a long time, but it is difficult to work with. Yet it has been recognized that if one were able to build an integrated circuit in gallium arsenide, we could probably get an improvement ranging from five to ten times, particularly in speed, over the performance of the best silicon circuit.

We recently built our first digital integrated circuits of gallium arsenide. We have entered into some contractual relationships with a number of computer manufacturers interested in this technology to give them the ultimate performance in super computers. We recently announced a contract with Cray Research, the builder of super computers or large-scale number crunching machines. Cray will be using gallium arsenide in the front end of those machines to give improved performance.

The second item on my list is the area of computer-aided design. This is another driving technology that I think will have great impact not only in the electronics areas of the 1980s and 1990s but also in all manufacturing industries where there is a complicated design process. We are seeing computers built out of integrated circuits being used to assist in the more rapid design and development of those very integrated circuits. The circle is closing.

Integrated circuits are being laid out using computer-aided design techniques. About four years ago a circuit could take us approximately 6,000 man hours to do design layout and to develop. Using these new techniques, we can do a similar circuit in approximately eighty hours. So we have reduced from 6,000 to eighty, almost a factor of a hundred, the amount of time and the amount of effort required. Of course we also enjoy the reliability and error-free operation that the computer provides us.

The use of computer-aided design obviously is not being limited to electronics. Much of our mechanical design is now being done in a computer-aided fashion. A Harris computer at General Motors, for example, is assisting in the design of automotive parts and automobiles themselves. Again, there are great time savings, because not only the actual layout is being computer aided, but also all of the different kinds of analyses that go along with it. Therefore, we are greatly increasing the productivity of the engineers in terms of being able to design new and better products.

Digital communications, we think, is going to be one of the driving technologies of the future. Again, the availability of basic digital building blocks and integrated circuits is allowing the application of these products to the communications area. Historically we have tended to deal with our information in what we've called analog form. That is, it's a signal which is time varying in an analog fashion. With digital communications, we are dealing with a digital signal: simply a series of ones and zeroes, or on and off, in which there is a numerical value given to the information being communicated or processed.

Now, obviously we live in an analog world, so why do we want to go to digital communications? Yet more and more of our transactions—in terms of the service industry, our engineering, and our industrial applications—are being done on the computer. The information is digital in nature. It is represented by numbers. And the communication of this information between computers, between users, and so forth, can be done more efficiently in digital format. Certainly it can be done more accurately. Having to transmit in analog form, converting everything from digital to analog and back to digital, is very difficult, inefficient, and relatively inaccurate. So the ability to communicate digitally, we believe, is a driving force in the business. It will continue to grow. What has slowed this process historically was the fact that digital circuitry was relatively expensive, but that is now coming down to the point where in memory circuits you can store great amounts of information at relatively low cost. There also is more bandwidth available by virtue of developments to allow you to transmit these relatively wide-band signals; the analog signals were a relatively narrow band.

So the use of digital technology even in telephone systems, I think, is just a matter of time. We and our competitors are now building PBXs that accommodate the use of digital telephony—digital transmission of computer-based information over telephone circuits.

Point-to-point communications offer other opportunities. A microwave system in London, for instance, is being used to transmit digital information from one point in the city to another, in both a voice and a computer-communications application.

High-level software is another driving technology. In the early days, of course, all of our software was written in what is called machine language. It was a very inefficient method of programming, very difficult to change. With time, we have gone to high-level languages that are relatively independent of the machines on which they are operating. They are much easier to use, they are more flexible, and they allow us to do more things with a computer than we could historically. We are now starting to develop machines to develop software. We are talking about a great deal of interaction between the man and the machine. We are talking about English-language programming; we're talking about the ability for machines to recognize and synthesize speech. There's a great deal of effort going on in this whole area of high level software, and I think that's going to be one of the driving technologies of the 1980s and 1990s.

Satellite communications will continue to have an impact in all of our businesses. There's no arguing that the application of satellite communications to our service industries is going to be very important. This is important not only domestically, but internationally for countries that have not had the communications infrastructure that exists in this country.

Satellite communications provide a very efficient, effective, and rapid means of building a communication system that allows the transmission of not only voice information, but video and television. That's why we are seeing rapid deployment of satellite communication systems of this type in Third World nations.

We're also seeing applications in terms of business communications. A major system being installed by Harris is a dedicated satellite communications network that will allow the Atlantic Richfield Corporation to tie together their domestic operations with their Alaskan operations. The system will have video teleconferencing capability, voice communication capability, and computer-to-computer capability. It will be one of the most sophisticated, most advanced dedicated satellite networks in the world when it goes into operation this year.

The technology is also moving very rapidly in terms of the frequency spectrum. One government satellite communications contract development Harris is working on uses the EHF (extremely high frequency) spectrum in which, as you move up in frequency, you can move down in size. We have built satellite antennas less than five inches in size. Consider the potential application of that technology in terms of rooftop or home antennas as we move up in the frequency spectrum. We also will have the advantage of less crowding, more band-width available, and the ability to transmit more digital information.

One type of technical data relay site antenna is being employed in the Space Shuttle program. To show you how far the technology has moved, this gold mesh antenna will unfurl in space and will maintain a surface accuracy of better than twenty-thousandths of an inch to a true parabola in space.

We are designing and building a 300-foot antenna for NASA for space deployment to provide improved space communications up into the year 2000. This is going to give us, again, the capability of having much smaller, less complex antennas on the ground and putting a lot of the complexity into space. This will be deployed by the Space Shuttle in the latter part of this decade.

Light wave systems, another very important driving technology for the 1980s and 1990s, use light as the communication medium. The advantages of light wave are that you can have a very high number of circuits on a single wire which are immune to electrical interference. You don't get the noise and the static that occur in an electromagnetic regime. You can have very high band widths, and it is relatively low in cost. It is indifferent to moisture and temperature, and you don't have short circuits with it. We are building a number of systems incorporating light wave for transmission, particularly of digital information. One system will have over a million voice circuits on a single cable.

All of these driving technologies are leading us to the fact that we are putting all of these things into an integrated communication network. Minicomputers, data terminals, mainframe computers, intelligent telephones, word processors, facsimile devices, video teleconferencing, digital PBXs—all are being tied together into something we call a local area network. Harris is working on products in all of these areas that will interact and work with each other in a local area network mode. Switch and access networks will allow you to get into the wide area networks using tandem switch and microwave systems. I talked about light wave systems, the public telephone links, radio telephone links— all are important parts of the switch and access network. They will connect into the wide area networks, made up of the public telephone, the value added networks, and the private satellite networks.

So we are going to see the proliferation of these networks. It's going to place a great deal of stress on companies such as ours to be sure of compatibility of our product lines to allow these things to work together in an integrated system.

Some of these driving technologies obviously introduce a large number of management challenges. One of the things we need to focus on is the excellence in management of industrial companies. We work very hard at maintaining a very strong technology capability. This means that we must spend heavily in research and development and this year we will spend something around $100 million of Harris money in addition to our government-sponsored research and development.

We work very hard to transfer government-sponsored technology into the commercial domain, because we think that is an important part of our strategy. It takes unusual organizational techniques and flexibility to manage these technology-based companies. We have tried to push down as far as we can into our divisional operating structure the responsibility for maintaining critical masses of people in these technology areas.

The people implications are very significant. We rely heavily upon the best and the brightest from our college and university systems to be able to follow and develop the technologies I have been describing.

In 1981, Harris alone hired over 1 percent of all new college graduates in engineering disciplines from the U.S. college and university system. We hire primarily electrical and computer science engineers. There has been much written and much discussion on the availability of adequate technical resources to support the industrial base of the future. It is a problem that is receiving national attention. But there is some question about whether we are going to be able to keep up with our international competitors.

One thing that worries many of us is the primary and secondary educational system and its lack of emphasis on math and the sciences. We worry whether it is providing the entering college students with the basics required to become the engineers and the scientists of the future. These technologies and this rapid rate of change place great stress on our organizational management techniques. That means we must continue to watch what is happening carefully. We must be flexible in terms of our planning process, in terms of our direction, our changes in direction—so it suggests that certain things will work in our kind of company and certain things won't.

What are the threats to the opportunities that these technologies present? I think there are several. Much has been said about international competition, particularly the Japanese. I think in the final analysis it means that U.S. industry must be able to compete on a fair and equitable basis with anyone in the world. I think we are prepared to do this. Part of the problem gets back to the definition of what constitutes fair and equitable competition.

Another question is the government's role in this whole process and whether the government is a help or a hindrance to what we are trying to achieve. That is also getting attention. I don't think governmental restrictions will be a fundamental limitation.

The need for excellence in our kind of business cannot be overstressed and I think many of us are working to improve on a continuing basis the overall effectiveness of our operations. One thing that needs some discussion and understanding also is the question of the impediments to excellence. My view is that excellence implies competition, it implies a winning and a losing process, it implies striving to be the very best. I think that we have seen too much complacency on the part of U.S. management in not being willing to compete on a worldwide basis effectively.

In our national work force we have seen a reluctance to base promotion and reward systems upon performance and excellence as opposed to other criteria. I think our university systems have contributed to the problem by some of their open admission policies. I refer to grade inflation and some relaxing of standards in performance. I think our government has contributed to this problem by confusing equality of opportunity with equality of results. All of these things, I think, have acted to slow down the rate of progress.

On the other hand, I think there's a great deal of attention being paid now to the need for excellence in organization and excellence in people. Certainly in our corporation we are giving it a great deal of focus and we think it is a very important aspect of the future success of our kind of business.

In summary, then, we think we are participating in markets that have great growth opportunities. The markets in which we participate are probably growing on average between 15 and 35 percent compounded annually. They average something around 20-percent compound growth. So we are in a very dynamic industry.

I think our success will be determined by how effectively we manage these companies and our standards for excellence in terms of our people, our products, and their quality. But the opportunity is a great one and I happen to be very optimistic about the future of our industry.

J. LELAND STRANGE

Microcomputer Enhancement: Challenges in an Exploding Industry

Let me tell you a little bit about Quadram, which two of us founded in September 1981.

My cofounder was Tim Farris, an engineer at City Spring Production. I brought to the company the finance and marketing experience and Tim brought the engineering and production skills. In December 1982, some fifteen months after Quadram was founded, we merged with Intelligent Systems Corp. Quadram's market value at the time of the merger was $35 million. Incidentally, today the market value is $75 million, so I'm not complaining about the merger. I assume that the market accepted it pretty well.

What had we done to warrant that kind of price? I'm not sure I know the complete answer. But I do know that in seventeen months we have introduced nineteen new products to the market. These are products that we designed in-house and manufactured in-house, not products we went out and bought from other people, although we plan to do some of that now. Since our start, we have designed and brought to market more than one product a month.

We have supported a number of leading microcomputer vendors, primarily the IBM personal computer and the Apple personal computer, in addition to making some other more generic type products.

I also know that what we brought to the table for the merger was a base of 900 retail dealers recruited in our first fifteen-month period. A year ago, we had only twelve people employed with us. Today we have 200. Does the high-tech industry do away with jobs? I don't know how to answer that question theoretically, but we are witness to the fact that this is one area of the business that has created many, many new jobs. We expect to have over 300 employees by March. Certainly that rate of growth is going to slow.

In terms of facilities, last year at this time we had one building of

3,000 square feet. We are now constructing a building of 60,000 square feet in the same office park.

Last March we did about $40,000 to $45,000 in sales. Since we are now a public company, we do not report sales by division; but this March it will be in the range of $3 million. We're running at an annual rate of about $36 million.

One of the difficulties we experienced in trying to manage this rapid growth occurred when we had to move to a new facility and couldn't keep up with product shipments.

We define the industry that we're in as being the "enhancement" industry. You probably have not seen that term too much. I define *enhancements* as a wide range of products that provide added value for the microcomputer user.

These products allow the user to enlarge the capacity and performance of the computer and to increase the number of applications for which the computer can be used. In effect, we trail whatever the microcomputer people do, simply enhancing their products.

Looking at enhancements generally, they include all those products that increase the value of a computer. Some examples might be modems, memory boards, buffers, peripheral interfaces, clocks, speech synthesizers, and storage devices. Monitors, printers, and certainly software are all enhancement products.

What is the size of the market? We see the micromarket growing at an average rate of 45 percent a year over the next five years. Incidentally, short-range and long-range planning are real problems for us with this kind of growth. Long-range planning is what we do after lunch; short-range is before. When I plan five years ahead, I'm going an awfully long way out for us.

We see the small-business market, which represents about 50 percent of the micromarket, as our major market. These are the people who need enhancements and can afford their price. We see the enhancement market growing at about double the rate of the microcomputer market. This may approach 100 percent a year.

Quadram has met the challenges of rapid growth primarily because we have had a marketing orientation. We have had a close connection between marketing and engineering. Neither engineering nor marketing decides on its own what kind of product to develop; it is a tight couple based on market needs and the ability to produce a product at a price that the market can accept. We are definitely market driven, not technology driven.

Let me offer an example of some of the problems in our industry in terms of marketing. Our major product is called a Quadboard. The latest issue of *PC World*, a personal computer magazine, carried eighteen full-page advertisements of goods that perform essentially the same function as our Quadboard. Three months ago there were just six ads. Today there are eighteen. I'll predict that in two months there will be thirty-six and I predict that next year there will be six again. All I want to do is be one of those six. A shakeout definitely is coming in that regard. For the short term, a lot of people are jumping into the market.

A Quadboard, incidentally, is a little printed circuit board designed to be inserted into an IBM personal computer. It will enhance the personal computer by giving it the additional capabilities that are built onto the board. These features are additional memory, the ability to interface with a modem or a printer, and an internal clock so you can time or date based on programming.

As part of our marketing orientation, we adopted a heavy advertising strategy. We went to the end users with large ads and gave them reasons, through a benefit orientation, why they should buy the product. Then we told them to contact our local dealer.

Now, when the first ad ran, there were no local dealers; but there were a lot of telephones that rang as a result of that ad and, consequently, we built a dealer base from that point on. We also used demand pricing. This industry is very tough to price. We priced our Quadboard a year ago at a level we have been able to maintain until this week. One year is a long time to build and maintain the same price in this business.

We look at the product life cycle for all our products. We think of a product life cycle as being six months. Obviously, many products are going to last two or three years, a long life cycle. But to keep from fooling ourselves as to what management has to do in the design phase, we say that every product has a life cycle of only six months. That keeps us on our toes.

Pricing and price erosion are going to account for many companies leaving this business. As of this next week, for instance, we are cutting the price of our Quadboard, which has been retailing for $595, down to $395. You don't nickel and dime it when you make price moves in this industry. They're pretty large moves.

Another major reason for our success in marketing has to do with the distribution channel. We chose to go to the retail market by using one-tier distribution, not by using two-tier distribution involving distributors. We went directly to retailers. That is the hard way to do it. It's the hard way to get sales. It takes you longer to get established.

But all of those things work in reverse, too. Once you're established, it's harder to be kicked off the shelf. You enjoy a one-to-one relationship with the retailers, as opposed to having the distributor try to recount what the retailer thought was said to the distributor. Consequently, we have close communication with the person who sells the product.

The other thing we've done in the retail area is to develop a wide product line. By having a number of products, we are able to take care of most requests made to a retailer relating to the major computers. Our objective is simply to be the only line of accessories or enhancements that the retailer needs. By having the widest line, we feel we can maintain the shelf space. We are in stores like Macy's, Bambergers, and Davison's, and those kinds of retail establishments do not change suppliers quickly. They have limited shelf space, and it's going to become a shelf space game.

I look at it a bit like marketing Tide or Cheer. I don't look at it as being anything special just because it's high tech, except for short product life cycles. It's strictly packaged goods; we do the same thing as all the other fellows do in the packaged goods business. It's the Procter & Gamble approach.

Another reason we think we have been successful is our fast response time. Again, since we have a large number of products, we've obviously had to react rapidly. Engineering must be able to turn out a product fast. This is difficult for engineers. They always want to overdesign, always want to take a little longer. It's the idea of perfection; they don't want to let it go. But we prefer immediate improvement as opposed to postponed perfection.

That is hard to teach to engineers, particularly those who come from other companies and who worked on their last project for two years. Then we turn around and say to them that we need a product in three months. It's a matter of getting the right products, but it may not have all the bells and whistles that you'll ever put on it. We try to get something out to market quickly.

In order to do that, you have to have decentralized decision making. One comment in Robert Waterman's book is his advice for action: do it, fix it, apologize later. I think we have that philosophy. Stated another way, it takes less time to apologize than to ask permission. It's a matter of everybody's taking action. The only way our 200 employees get in trouble with us is to not be doing something, not taking action. They'll never get in trouble for doing the wrong thing if they use a reasonable, rational process to get there.

We are flexible in our decision making. We don't say that everything has to be built in-house, even though everything to date has been. We are a market-driven company so we will sell products that are developed outside. We have lots of personal computers in our shop, probably 40 or 50, which means that people can get information quickly. They can't ever say the data processing department told them it would take three months to do that. You just do it yourself, with no excuses.

We also emphasize productivity through people; we certainly have the entrepreneurial philosophy because we are a relatively young company and that philosophy is easy to maintain at this point. We do encourage the growth of individuals. Those are not just words to which we give lip service. It's something we practice.

A little example happened last week. One of the women who does the budgeting came up and gave me the budget I was taking to a planning meeting. She said, "I wouldn't bet my life that all the numbers are exactly right." I handed it back to her and said, "You are fixing to bet my life that it's right because I'm not going to look at it before I hand it out." The message is not to expect someone above you to correct your mistakes. You do it. She took it back, found a couple of mistakes, and gave it back to me. I didn't look at it when I handed it out.

That is the kind of thing we are trying to do with people. We allow them creativity; we allow them to make decisions. Some of the decisions I don't like. A lot of the decisions I wouldn't make. But the only option we had was to stifle creativity, which consequently would have stifled our growth. That's why we like to see lots of things happening, even though lots of mistakes may transpire as a result. Again, to quote Robert Waterman, "Let people make mistakes." We've made our share and we intend to keep making lots and lots of mistakes because that means we're doing things and trying things.

In terms of hiring, we typically look for generalists. We can't do that in engineering, of course, but we can in most of the other areas of the organization. We are looking for good people and it doesn't matter what area they are in because they're going to move anyway. It is seldom that someone who starts in budgeting stays in budgeting.

Another major factor in our business is cost effectiveness. We look at the enhancement business as being something that eventually will be driven by cost.

Certainly the Japanese competition is a factor. We purchase very aggressively. We do variance monitoring, very religiously and very quickly, at the end of each month. All budgeting is zero based and we draw up completely new budgets every quarter. We justify everything every quarter instead of on an annual basis.

We allow a lot of decision making within the budgeting guidelines. Someone mentioned the Procter & Gamble philosophy of having one-page memos. We don't want any memos. We ask, why did you give me this? Why do I need to see this? Do it. It's the idea, again, of action.

For a small company, our planning process is a bit unusual. When we were a very small company, we did all the things that the billion-dollar company does. I think it has paid off. We had a very well-defined value, mission, and objective statement. We knew early what we were about in terms of values and where we were headed. Knowing where we are going has helped us as we bring in new people.

Our hiring always lags our needs. We never hire in anticipation, always after. We let the structure follow the strategy. As a matter of fact, probably we would have less structure even today if it weren't for the outside world. We really had a triumvirate in terms of management until we talked about merging and securing venture capital. We found that venture capitalists didn't like the kind of hats we were wearing. Therefore, we put together a little organizational structure that we showed them, while we kept operating our own way inside.

The truth is that this is still the way it goes. The only way to manage growth is to let decision making take place a little bit outside the structure. You're going to have a little chaos. We accept it as part of doing business. We accept it as part of what is required to get the growth that we want.

We have an informal system of interdepartmental communications. The communications process is probably the most difficult thing we have had to cope with in our growth. Let me give some examples of what we have gone through in fighting the proliferation of memos. We asked our six marketing managers to get together every day at 11:30 for five minutes to pass information. That didn't work because every other day three of them would be out of town. Three people would go to the meeting, but no one else would show up.

The next thing we suggested was that, if you wanted to have a meeting, you would post it on the bulletin board. The sign would just say, "meeting." If there were people outside the group that you wanted to come, you would put their names on it. That worked for about three weeks. About four other attempts have been made to find a way to get around the communications jungle. One of them eventually is going to work. I wish I could announce today how we solved the problem, but I can't.

Still, we like to do things our way as opposed to accepting how everyone on the outside says something has to be done. I can remember when we were operating at an annual rate of $5 million, the bankers were saying, "You can't do it this way." At the $10 million annual rate, they said, "You can't do it this way, you can't double." They're saying the same thing today. I'm sure there is a point where you can no longer do it that way but until we can prove we can't, we're going to continue.

A consistent value system by top management that has been given to every employee from Day One definitely has helped. We stress the efforts of the organization. We stress respect for people and their individual growth. We could not pay high salaries, so what we did was find people who wanted something more than money. They wanted to be part of a dynamic, growing organization. Now they want money.

We adopted a symbol, two Q's for "Quadram Quality," and have tried to push that through the organization. You can talk about quality all day long. A lot of companies talk about it and never really achieve it.

They think all you have to do is talk about it. We would not publish our Quadram Quality symbol until we reached a certain level of returns. Everybody knew internally that, until we got down to a ½ percent return rate, the two Q's would not go out in our advertising. Rather than going out and making claims we couldn't fulfill, we had to become something and then communicate what we were. Hype without substance really is nothing. You get caught up with the hype.

The other value that has been added by management is a consumer-marketing orientation. It is not just in the marketing function, not just in the engineering function, but throughout our organization. A lot of people, including technical support employees, report to marketing. We select one person off the production floor for every trade show. We will participate in nineteen trade shows this year, so nineteen people who normally stuff parts on a slide line, will go to a show. When they come back, they can tell people on the slide line what the company is about from a different kind of perspective.

Our two receptionists are both off the slide line. The movement throughout the company is evident. It's possible to move at Quadram.

I mentioned our planning process. We do a fair amount of planning although it's quick and there's not a lot of paperwork to back it up. We certainly have plenty of challenges. We have the challenge to maintain the competitive edge that we have now. Incidentally, we feel that we have in excess of a 50-percent market share in our major products.

It's our job to continue coming up with products that will allow us to maintain a dominant position in the industry. It's also our job to maintain Quadram Quality in terms of service, products, and people. In terms of managing growth, we are going to let the chaos continue. Maybe we'll be able to report back next year on just how big a company can grow and still remain a chaotic organization.

DISCUSSION

WINER: I'm Leon Winer, and I'm with Pace University, New York City. Can you explain the specific benefits of buying a Quadboard versus buying an IBM board for the IBM personal computer?

STRANGE: IBM doesn't really make a competitive product. The key to our Quadboard was recognizing the market need early after IBM introduced its personal computer. A Quadboard has four different functions on a single board. IBM has limited slots for expansion.

To accomplish what you can accomplish with one of our boards, you would have to purchase four different IBM boards. So it's price plus the ability to leave other slots open and free if you purchase Quadboards instead of the IBM boards.

We are talking about a board that would add an additional 256K memory to an IBM. It would add a serial interface board. It would add a parallel board and also a clock calendar.

KOCH: What is the limit to this growth? And how do you go through the shakeout and emerge as one of the survivors?

STRANGE: As to growth, we are limited by what happens in the microcomputer field. We simply follow the microcomputers.

Certainly changes in the microcomputer field will change the way you perceive a micro in the next three, four, or five years. But regardless of those changes, there will always be the necessity for different kinds of enhancements. Whatever limit you can put on microcomputer growth is the limit you would put on enhancement growth. In the terms of shakeout, that game is being played now. I think the shakeout game is totally dependent upon market penetration today, shelf space gained today, and reputation gained this year— 1983.

It will be much more difficult for a new entrant to be successful in the marketplace because now it's a marketing game and not a technology game. We're not on the leading edge of technology. We take what other companies do and try to find a way to use those in our particular marketplace.

KOCH: Why don't the computer giants say, "That is an exciting market, I want my share of it?"

STRANGE: Why don't IBM or Apple or the other computer makers do it? The fact is they're trying to get the enhancements market now. They always have. Go back historically and look at what's happened with Apple or Hewlett-Packard. Many, many modems have been hung on Hewlett-Packard's computers, but most of those have not been purchased from Hewlett-Packard even though HP sells a modem. The reason is that the microcomputer manufacturing firm is also running as fast as it can run. What it has to be concerned with is selling what we call the "mother board," the base machine.

If a firm is buying fifty pages of advertising space this month in a magazine, its executives are trying to decide what to put on their pages. It's awfully difficult for the vice president in charge of peripherals to request five pages for a little peripheral board that sells for $300 when that page could be utilized for a $3,000 machine.

It's a matter of focus. The manufacturer has to focus on its bread and butter, whereas our focus is strictly the enhancement business.

HARTLEY: Clearly, the edge that a company like Quadram enjoys is that it's very flexible, very fast on its feet, and very focused. It's difficult for any company, no matter its size—the IBMs of the world or Harris or Pitney Bowes— to be all things to all people. There are going to be marketing niches out there and the clever and innovative firms are going to find those niches. If they have the capability to exploit them, then I think they will be successful.

Quadram has defined clearly the strategy that I think could be successful in that kind of marketplace.

My guess is that one of the advantages Quadram has is that in a short period of time it has brought to the marketplace very competitive technological products and also has done an excellent job of marketing.

I think this combination of strong technology based in a marketplace drive, which we all try for, is a winning combination no matter the size. Once you get past the critical mass, that is all that is required.

HEBEL: I'm Tom Hebel with Flagship Bank of Okeechobee, Florida. A lot of people, of course, will never have a personal computer. At what point do you think most homes will have some kind of terminal tied in with banks and stores, and what are you doing to participate in that?

STRANGE: At what point? I would hate to hazard a guess that we will all be part of that. I do think, though, that at some point we all will have a personal computer or some type of tie-in. What we are doing to tie in is working with things such as videotex cards that can be put on an IBM or Apple. Again, we follow the major computer companies and develop enhancements. Incidentally, if anybody knows what Japanese computer company is going to win out I wish he or she would let me know. We would like to start building enhancements for it.

KOCH: Home banking is one exciting area for personal computers and we find there are probably some fifteen experiments going on around the nation. I anticipate a legitimate consumer demand for these products where you'll have a personal computer or some black box in your home and you will be able to dial up and do all your banking. Cox Cable has an exciting system called the Home Serve System that has signed up banks throughout the nation.

The economics now make it very real. The economics are as low as paying for Home Box Office. It is also cost efficient.

My sense is that within twenty-four months you will see a lot of these things in the marketplace for consumers just like cable TV was five years ago. It's terribly simple technology. Any bank with a computer system that allows you to dial up and transfer information can install a home system quickly.

JAMES L. BAST

Automated Office Equipment:
Will Rapid Growth Continue?

Office automation is both a cause and an effect of the current requirements of today's business world. Technology is causing office automation itself to move faster, and this feeds management needs in a positive
manner. What's more, management is being required to work smarter
and more productively, so the effect is to seek even more automation.
As managers, we are constantly faced with the double-edged sword of
paper. On the one hand, we need lots of data, but there is so much
paper that we cannot handle it. On the other hand, there is not enough
real information out of the data to help us determine the true impact
and meaning of the data presented to us.

At Dictaphone, we have been helping people work smarter since 1923,
which was the inception of voice processing and dictation tools to make
office workers more productive. Dictaphone, the number one name in
dictation, reported revenues of $175 million last year. Our 3,800 em-
ployees around the world are helping people understand that office automation can mean simple dictation or highly sophisticated word processing.

Dictaphone is a subsidiary of Pitney Bowes, a $1.5 billion company,
252nd in the Fortune 500 list of U.S. industrial firms. In 1982, every
financial performance factor of Pitney Bowes improved, demonstrating
in part the value of a company being in the office automation field.
Dictaphone merged with Pitney Bowes in 1979. In 1980, it went into
word processing through the acquisition of a small but premier word
processing company. In 1982, our growth increased strongly in word
processing, despite the slower economy, with award-winning products
and strong customer support. An exciting new product announcement
by Dictaphone in 1982 in text-editing systems presented one of the first
natural language capabilities on word processors shown to the industry.

The industry in which we participate generally can be characterized
as U.S. office equipment manufacturers. It is a dynamic growth indus-

try, which last year grew about 25 to 30 percent in word processing, and has enjoyed a 14-percent compounded growth rate over the last five years. Although it was slowed somewhat by the recession, it grew faster than most other U.S. industries. Obviously, fierce competition exists among the many companies in the industry and from potential participants outside the United States who would like to share in our markets.

A valid question would be, Is the past prologue for the future? I certainly intend to provide the answer to that question. To help do that I will frame the factors affecting our office equipment industry and will let you make some of your own decisions as I provide the information.

I interpret office automation as "improving efficiencies and effectiveness of office workers through applied use of electronic systems." Notice that the focus is on the workers themselves, what they are doing and the problems confronting them, rather than on actual hardware or products.

It is clear that office automation came somewhat after factory automation. The emphasis in the early 1950s and 1960s was on data processing, using high-speed mainframe computers in a centralized location. They were driven by data processing specialists, rather than information management people as they are more commonly called today.

In the 1970s, the thrust turned toward word processing. The typewriter evolved into printer-based and then into display-based word processors, using centralized or decentralized systems. The primary focus was to make secretaries and clerical workers more productive.

In the 1980s, the personal computer is making a revolutionary thrust into the business environment. It focuses on managers and professionals, who previously have been deprived of adequate tools, by providing effective price or performance products to interest them. It further emphasizes the fact that we are now an information-based society.

Up to now, office automation generally has been implemented as single-function products. Word processors, for example, are used primarily for text editing, and personal computers mainly for spreadsheet analysis. The next step already is gaining speed in 1983: a broader emphasis, heightened by a multiplicity of functions, and greater interconnection of devices. Internally, work groups will be able to share data and information, and externally more communications will result from lower costs and higher speeds. New features such as graphics and color are proliferating, all stimulating office knowledge workers' interest in using these modern systems.

Part of the reason for the shift to management focus is the changing nature of our work force. The growth of white-collar workers in the United States has been more than twice that of blue-collar workers. The white-collar group now numbers over 51 million, a significant marketplace for many products. Within the white-collar group are more than 5 million secretaries, 11 million managers, and 16 million professionals, most of whom have been virtually ignored in previous productivity directions. In addition, these people are better educated, with higher expectations for advancement and quality of work life.

The pressure on profits is tremendous. In 1981, $1 trillion was spent on office-based white-collar workers—of which 75 percent represented salaries—and only 10 percent came from the information industry. Only $1,200 was spent each year per knowledge worker on such work tools as telephones, word processors, personal computers, and other information products.

The technological evolution is providing fairly rapid change. Higher volumes and new technologies are combining to drive equipment prices dramatically downward. Sizes are decreasing extremely fast. We have moved quickly from large-scale integration of electronics to very large scale integration. VLSI itself will be surpassed by further technological developments, resulting in a continuing improvement in price and performance. This, in turn, will foster greater usage of data and information by all office workers. Virtually all office products are affected, from simple copiers and calculators to sophisticated new terminals and communication devices.

The economics of our businesses force us to be aware of the external effects of competition—companies that are improving their capabilities, whether they are from the United States, Japan, Germany, or other nations. Our responsiveness to customers' expectations and our own needs for decision information direct our attention to these imperatives.

A study of office productivity improvement programs indicates that a 10-percent increase in effectiveness resulting from such programs could save more than $95 billion in this country each year. This can be obtained only through improved communication links, using common data bases and more rapid communication for time-sensitive information. The role of the PBX in office automation itself is driving companies toward more joint ventures and recognition of the telephone exchange as the hub of the office.

Responding to those imperatives, office equipment manufacturers and system integrators are providing directions that will move everyone quickly to multifunction workstations. The acceptance of both word processing and personal computing is setting the stage for convergency and integration of functions like word processing, voice processing, communications, and data processing. Use of artificial intelligence and natural language will make all of these items more acceptable for white-collar workers.

When I use the term *multifunction workstation,* my definition is "a device capable of performing more than one function, directed to several types of office workers." I don't intend to get into the subtle differences between executive workstations, professional workstations, professional computers, personal computers, and other devices. However, multifunction workstations are those that generally include several specific functions, including intelligent telephone capabilities, dictation, word processing, computing, calendaring, electronics, and voice mail. They will be designed primarily to have a small footprint on the professional's desk, and to be used for multitasking in his or her environment.

The price and performance capabilities of such workstations and their technology improvements will match with the versatility of users as they seek both convenience and user-friendly interfaces with their work environment.

Such workstations are being introduced initially as generic offerings like a smart telephone. They will quickly be tailored to specialized user functions, discriminating between, for example, an executive who needs to view information often and an analyst who may want to calculate data more frequently. The smart telephone will yield to the intelligent telephone, with different functions provided for people who might be at the top of the company or in the financial area or in the billing area, just to name three examples.

Functionality will also be directed toward specialized industry applications, whether it be banking, legal, manufacturing, insurance, or others. The size of the work group will be influential in the types of multifunction workstations required. Stand-alone systems will be different from those used in larger groups, where sharing of large files and high-speed printers will be required.

One of the key functional areas provided by such products will be voice processing, which includes dictation and voice mail. As we in Dictaphone have pointed out in the past, if executives used machine dictation equipment, they generally would increase their daily time for decision making by thirty to sixty minutes. But beyond dictation, voice processing will incorporate enhanced capabilities such as digital voice, voice store and forward, and annotation of text.

Speech recognition will move rapidly from the limited discrete recognition of about 100 words to continuous speech recognition. Following by five to ten years we could see a capability to provide hard copy or to screen copy strictly from speech without a secretary's entering it on a keyboard. The main thrust will be to make the systems easier to use, and to get away from keyboard fright that is holding back some executives from participating in the office automation phenomenon.

Another key area of the multifunction workstation will be the interconnection links between people. Local area networks for internal connections will vary between broadband and baseband applications, depending on whether voice or data predominates in the internal environment. External communication will improve in both speed and ease of use, helped by technologies in microwave and satellite communications.

The yield from these developments for all of us in office automation will be increased efficiencies. Knowledge work will be done increasingly in the home. It is estimated that by 1990 or 1992 the home information services industry will be a $12 billion to $15 billion industry. The term *cottage industry* already is familiar, and executives are hearing more and more about carrying their office in a briefcase so they can work in many places.

The demand for increased efficiencies and use of such workstations is enormous. The driving forces are office population, rising salaries, and declining product costs, combined with increased performance capabilities. It is interesting that such devices' penetration of the work environment is currently low. Fewer than 3 percent of all managers today have display-based workstations. By 1986, it is anticipated that this will have increased to only 8 percent, and half of the secretaries still will not have display-based word processing products at their desks. The implication of the driving forces coupled with low penetration rates is that the shipments of dedicated stand-alone word processors and personal computers will level off but the growth rate of multifunction workstations will continue to accelerate and to feed a receptive marketplace.

Will rapid growth in automated office equipment continue? The answer is clearly yes. I estimate that annual unit growth will continue faster than 30 percent, with slower growth in dollars as the price and performance improvements continue to take effect in a less inflationary environment. The office automation equipment industry is responding to the many needs of the marketplace for increased information in a more time-sensitive manner. I think there is tremendous opportunity for an American resurgence over Japanese and other imports, not solely because of greater software strength, but because of our willingness to be more innovative over the long run.

Challenges definitely lie ahead for the industry. But personally I am tired of the criticism that the United States has lost competitive advantage because we are too much oriented toward the quick buck, to low risk and sexy hype on new bells and whistles rather than to real productive products with real benefits to users. We will need some help in this area, including less government regulation. The government must provide more incentives for capital formation in all of our industries, particularly in some of our new technologies. I am most optimistic about companies and the industry in which we are participating. I am also completely sure that we in the white-collar area will be achieving greater productivity than we have experienced in the past.

DISCUSSION

FEINBERG: Bob Feinberg, House Banking Committee. I saw an article that discussed the rapid increase in the number of circuits that can be put on a chip, but then concluded that this growth is proceeding so rapidly that it's becoming impossible to test these chips to find out whether the logic works or not. The conclusion was not so pessimistic as to say it can't be done but identified it as a serious problem the semiconductor industry has to confront. Would any of you gentlemen express your views on that issue?

HARTLEY: That observation is correct: It is a very real problem in our industry. I'd say the technology for design and processing these circuits has exceeded the technology for testing them. We spend a great deal of time, money, and effort to test these devices; and we are, of course, trying to solve that problem. The ultimate solution is actually computer-aided design of the test programs. We are moving rapidly now to a point where, once the design is completed by the computer-aided design system, automatically a computer-driven test program will be generated.

BAST: The reality is that we have to provide the solutions. If you buy a product that doesn't work, you will tell eleven of your friends that it's a dog and they shouldn't buy it. If you get a good product and it works, you may tell three of your friends that it works. None of us in the industry can afford to have that kind of an 11-to-3 ratio working against us. We have found internally that the testing has to be done to bring in products that work and are user friendly. I've become a bug killer, I guess, in going after those bugs in software that are highly elusive but that must be found. I think the technology will follow as rapidly as necessary to keep up.

KOCH: Although complementary metal oxide semiconductor (CMOS) technology was introduced in the early 1970s, it has only recently become popular for use in consumer products. If I understand correctly, the high density and low power requirements of CMOS chips allow consumer electronic products, such as television sets or fluorescent lighting, to be reduced in size and to be more energy efficient. Can you explain the applications of CMOS technology?

HARTLEY: As you observed, the technology has been around for awhile. But while the technology was well understood in the early 1970s, the reduction to practice was very difficult. Many of the leading manufacturers in this country decided that the problems would never be solved and, therefore, left it to Harris and a couple of others to pursue what they saw as a dead-end technology. It turns out their pessimistic predictions weren't correct and that only we in this country and the Japanese adopted CMOS technology as a mainstream technology.

Unfortunately, the Japanese embraced it totally and from almost a zero market penetration in the late 1970s they now have well over 50-percent market penetration.

So it has moved to be a mainstream technology in spite of the difficulties in processing. Harris is probably the leading CMOS technology processor in the United States. To answer your question with regard to benefits, the reason, of course, we pursued it so aggressively is that it has great benefits for the user. It has very low power. It allows very high packing densities on a circuit, and we believed that the cost could be brought down to the point where it would be priced competitively with more conventional, so-called NMOS technology and bipolar technology. That has, in fact, come to pass. I think that by the late 1980s we will see more than 50 percent of all integrated circuits being manufactured with this technology.

CHENG: Dinah Cheng with Union Carbide Corporation. You mentioned that gallium arsenide can give five to ten times better performance than silicon. I don't know if you are aware that Union Carbide is building a polycrystaline silicon plant in Washington. We are supposed to be able to produce a silicon that is going to enable a much improved performance, so I wonder if you could comment on this.

My other question is: Could you tell us the difference between light wave and fiber optics, because a lot of the characteristics seem to be similar.

HARTLEY: I did not mean to suggest that silicon was an outmoded technology or that it would not be with us for years to come. In fact, Union Carbide and others are working, as are the users such as Harris, on making silicon a more effective base material for building integrated circuits. I think it will remain the mainstream for many years to come. I think silicon has a great future and that a great percentage of the products being built in silicon operate perfectly well in the speed ranges where the applications don't require ultra-performance.

But there is a fundamental physical phenomenon at work here, called electron mobility, and electron mobility is much greater in gallium arsenide. Fundamentally, that means things can move faster through it and, therefore, ultimately you can build faster circuits.

Our users in the computer industry are all speed driven, wanting to process more instructions per second. They want to perform more computations per second on a continuing basis. So I think we will begin to see the very large scale machines including some portion of gallium arsenide late in the 1980s. We will see more and more of this with time, but gallium arsenide will not replace silicon.

Addressing your second question, the difference between fiber optics and light wave, I did not make that point clear. They are synonymous. In light wave communications, the medium in which that light is transmitted is fiber optics. This is a very fine quality of glass fiber that allows the transmission of light with relatively low loss over long distances. Fiber optics, then, are an integral part of the light wave system.

METZKER: Paul Metzker, Federal Reserve Bank of Atlanta. Could you address the future for storage technologies? Most of your discussion is concentrated on memory and the chip technology involved in the actual computation process; but a lot of the things I see refer to going from floppy disks into hard disks with personal computers and some day possibly into laser disk storage and things of that nature.

KOCH: In addition to that, please discuss holographic technology and holographic storage. You did a lot of pioneering work in that area.

HARTLEY: Several years ago, most forecasters were writing off silicon as a storage medium—that is, the use of integrated circuits to store large amounts of information—basically because of cost reasons. But then we saw the 64,000-element memory circuit random access memory, and now people are coming out with 128,000 and 256,000 storage elements on a single chip. The prices are entirely competitive and the speeds are far greater than any other memory technique around today. I suspect that trend will continue.

I know the industry currently is working on a 1 million storage element integrated circuit. Now, that's not to say the other technologies, the rigid and floppy disks, won't continue to play an important role. I believe they will. Their access speed—that is, the speed at which you can get to the information and bring it back and use it—is somewhat slower. Yet it is perfectly adequate for a number of applications, and it is much cheaper than other forms of technology.

I think the magnetic disks and the integrated circuit memory, the solid state memories, are going to be the tool to driving things. Bubble memories were mentioned early on as a revolutionary technique that was going to take over the marketplace. That has not come to pass. The progress made in silicon simply bypassed bubble memories and most people now are relegating them to a limited number of applications.

When you get to very large archival storage, for example, holographic or other optical techniques for storing the digital information are exciting possibilities. We now have memories that can store the Library of Congress in a small machine and can access it relatively rapidly.

So, why isn't everyone using that technology? The real problem with it is it isn't what is called a "read, write, and read again" type of memory. An off-line system is required to construct the memory, and it is not easily erasable or changed. It is more useful where you have archival or permanent storage requirements. But it is relatively inexpensive. Many people who have legal requirements for storing documents, such as insurance companies and banks, are very interested in holographic techniques for large memory storage.

KOCH: The multidimensional holographic storage is probably the most exciting sort of storage device for the 1990s and into the future. It captures every single point from three or four different sides; it is completely dimensional.

RUSSELL: I am Jim Russell with the *Miami Herald*. One of our most widely embraced national priorities seems to be to create more jobs. Some of the technologies you are talking about would tend to eliminate some jobs, but would create others in new industries. Are we going to eliminate more jobs than we create as these technologies develop?

BAST: The big scare of the computer introductions was that thousands of jobs would be eliminated. What's really happened is that those jobs have been displaced. With an information-based society we need more information and, therefore, we create more jobs for people to pull it out of data. Even though secretaries become more effective on word processing devices, there has been no decrease in the number of secretarial jobs. So I think we're enhancing people's ability to work effectively. When they do that, the jobs are not being put at risk by the technologies of our society.

HARTLEY: I agree absolutely. We are making it possible for less-skilled information workers to perform relatively sophisticated functions by using new types of machines. We're also seeing a phenomenon in which the very rapid growth and application of these products creates more jobs within manufacturing industries. With the increase in technology, people want to incorporate that technology into more and more sophisticated products, circuits, or whatever.

So this driving force tends to introduce new products and to require more people. For example, our employment has been growing, not as fast as our company certainly, but within an 8- to 12- percent compound growth rate per year.

AVANTI: I'm Tom Avanti with Ethyl Corporation. You clarified the question about the relationship between silicon and gallium arsenide. Would you expand a little, though, on the concept that light might perhaps replace electrons in the future? If so, when would this possibly take place and what would be the implications on material suppliers?

HARTLEY: The timing with regard to this application is now. An article in *Fortune* less than a year ago described the new so-called eastern corridor trunk telephone link, which is being installed now. There was hot competition between U.S. industry and the Japanese to supply this particular system, which is totally light wave based. It is not a copper cable or a series of bundles of cables being strung from Boston to Washington, but rather a light wave system. Three or four years ago, we put in a 60-mile Canadian system for Alberta Telephone which was entirely a light wave system. It could carry over 500,000 telephone circuits on that one system. So the applications are here today.

We're also beginning to see a lot of applications and interest in this as a technique for computer-to-computer communications. We are already supplying a light wave connecting link with many of our computer-based products. I suspect that in the not too distant future, probably in the next ten-year time span, we will begin to see offices wired with fiber optic cable as well as coaxial cable. I think that is coming. Again, I don't think it's going to displace the conventional technologies; it will be an expansion of those technologies.

KOCH: When will we begin seeing this cellular technology in public use? When will we be able to walk around with inexpensive satellite-driven two-way communication devices that will allow us to talk as if we were on a telephone?

HARTLEY: The technology is in place now to implement a program such as that. The Federal Communications Commission has given approval for the embryonic system of that type, the so-called cellular system, which will allow automobile and home telephones to be interconnected within a geographical area. Those systems should start to come on line, I think, in the 1986–1987 period.

With regard to satellite systems, the government is now working on a program called a global positioning system. We in industry—and Harris is playing an important role in this—are developing such a system, in which a man, a tank, a vehicle, an aircraft, or a ship at sea can determine its absolute position within one foot—within one meter, actually.

If and when this system goes into mass production, it will introduce a number of new applications. We can envision navigation information being presented in automobiles and road maps. With regard to satellite communications tied into the portable radio, I think we're looking at the 1990s.

LEVINSON: Marc Levinson, Bureau of National Affairs. You made reference to the need for some sort of antitrust exemption or other special preference to enable you to do the necessary research and development in the future. Would you elaborate on that a bit? Specifically, do you think it is going to be necessary for competitors to do research jointly in this field?

BAST: Legislation to achieve that is pending now on Capitol Hill. It's being driven in part by the chairman of Control Data and other corporations who are saying that for the United States to take a different posture than the totally subsidized Japanese development society, we should be able to work together effectively at the research stage. I think we should be able to accomplish that without slowing down competition or creating other problems that the federal government has to worry about.

HARTLEY: A corporation has been formed called MCC, Microelectronics and Computer Technology Corporation. Ten companies including Harris chartered the corporation to pursue advanced technologies on a joint basis. It has been reviewed by the Justice Department, which has given a preliminary finding that it is not anticompetitive.

The basic purpose of this program is to provide a vehicle for pooling research and development resources that could then be applied by the individual companies in a competitive product arena. So there will be no product development work, only technology development that these ten corporations will share before we have at it in the open marketplace. We consider this a sensible approach to trying to meet some of the government sponsorship in foreign countries in which there is a closer tie and not the same antitrust laws or market-oriented system that exists in this country.

Let me add that the secret to transferring technology is basically in people. We've found there is no substitute for moving technology from one place to another. You have to do it by means of people. You can't just publish data and give them specifications. In one joint-venture operation we conducted with Matra in France, we actually had their people resident in our plants for some two years and we've had our people over there. That's the basic technique we have used.

BAHARY: I'm Emil Bahary with American Bell. Could you comment on the close working relationship of firms with universities and also comment on some of the dangers of doing that, as far as integrity of education goes?

HARTLEY: It's a very good question and I think a very important one. We in industry should be doing everything we can, and Harris is trying to do its share, to encourage the universities to undertake programs that will help to advance the state of the technology and the state of knowledge and also serve as a vehicle for training the bright young men and women that we need for the future.

There are several mechanisms for doing this. One of the most important is cash—the fact that we are willing to support an institution financially through grants and gifts, or by giving equipment. It is also important to establish close working relationships. We now have programs under way in which we have people resident at MIT. We have another program with Berkeley, where we have researchers in residence. We are actually interchanging with Berkeley; their researchers come down and work with us, exchanging ideas and information.

What are the dangers and the problems? The basic problem is competition. The universities have, and I guess properly so, the conviction that one must share knowledge with the whole world. Of course, we in industry are very jealous of our competitive edge in terms of proprietary technological position. That's not an insurmountable problem. We've been able to work around that. There are certain things we agree we won't share and certain things we will. This is an obligation for us in industry and we ought to be doing more of it.

WINSTON: I am Jim Winston from Florida. You seem comfortable that we are at least looking at the educational problem. We've all read that we are graduating a hundred lawyers to every one in Japan, yet we graduate fewer engineers. Can you expand on what we are doing and what you think the results will be?

HARTLEY: Maybe if we shut down some of the law schools, that would help. The system works, but the problem is the lag. We in industry are interested in hiring the bright young engineers and computer science graduates and are paying them high starting salaries. The word has gotten around and the deans of the various schools, such as the University of Florida and Georgia Tech, say they have more applications for engineering school than they have had at any time in the last ten years. In fact, their problems now are servicing them by providing faculty and staff.

So the word is out that there's a great opportunity in the engineering profession, and this is attracting some of the good people that we need. But the problem is, of course, that there is a four- to six-year lag in terms of the needs of the industry. Will it be adequate to service the needs? It's going to be touch and go, but I think it will be adequate.

RIECK: My name is Steve Rieck with the Georgia Department of Community Affairs. Being a former military man, I found that the best way to protect communications was to hard wire between units rather than run the risk of radio interference. In your opinion, are adequate measures being taken both to protect the investment in the hardware involved in satellite communications and to protect them from physical damage or other interference that might occur in the future?

HARTLEY: That's a matter of some concern to many of us, particularly those who are in the government side of satellite communications as well as the commercial-industrial side. With regard to security of the information being transmitted, much of it is not secured. It is easily intercepted by anyone who wants access to that information.

I might hasten to add, however, that much of our domestic telephone traffic is transmitted over point-to-point microwave. All it takes to pick up that telephone conversation is a simple receiver. So we have less security in this country in terms of privacy of information than most people really understand.

This problem is being addressed by people in the military side by coming up with techniques for encoding or encrypting the information. And I think we are going to see more and more of this as we become more and more dependent upon computer-based data systems. The Federal Reserve Board has been very concerned about this question of voice security. Harris has supplied to the System a secure voice encryption system that maintains voice recognition yet still has the security that is absolutely necessary. More will be done in regard to the question of privacy.

With regard to the physical security of the satellite system, the only unsettling part has to do with outright hostility, war, and the vulnerability of the satellites. While they can be hardened and they can be protected, they are not invulnerable. That suggests you must have a backup system.

INTRODUCTION OF SPEAKER

William F. Ford

Virtually all of us, in business and in government, agonize regularly over the problems of predicting what may happen tomorrow, or next week. For your business, the challenge may be projecting the changes that you see emerging today and translating them into the market opportunities of tomorrow.

Alvin Toffler, author and social critic, has built a worldwide reputation by looking at the trends shaping up today and projecting those developments into the future. Toffler, who is best known for his analyses of contemporary social change, first coined the term future shock in a 1965 article. The term became the title of his 1971 best seller and has passed quickly into common usage. Toffler defines the term as "the shattering stress and disorientation that we induce in individuals by subjecting them to too much change in too short a time."

While Future Shock described the personal and social costs of rapid change, his 1980 work—The Third Wave—sought to reduce those costs by providing a framework for understanding tomorrow's society. His historical synthesis, built on the metaphor of "colliding waves of change," offers an optimistic response to that onrushing future shock that he warned us about.

What does all that mean? Toffler tells us that we have begun to enter a Third Wave of social evolution that will supplant the two previous waves—a First Wave based on agriculture and a Second Wave that arrived with the Industrial Revolution. He will touch on those "waves" of evolution in his presentation.

The popularity of Toffler's eye-opening volumes has given his ideas a worldwide forum. They have been published in some thirty languages around the world, from French, German, Spanish, and

Japanese to Turkish, Hebrew, Arabic, Chinese, and Polish. Yet the ideas in The Third Wave *were considered so revolutionary that publication was banned in Poland when military authorities cracked down in 1981. The book also remains on the banned list in Saudi Arabia.*

His work has been recognized in the United States with the Mc-Kinsey Foundation Book Award for "distinguished contributions to management literature." It also has been honored in France and other countries. His books frequently are required reading on university campuses from the United States and Japan to Brazil and Zaire. They are studied by government officials around the globe and have drawn comment from world leaders ranging from Richard Nixon to Pierre Trudeau and Indira Gandhi.

ALVIN TOFFLER

Toward a Third Wave Economy

If the invention of farming 10,000 years ago set off the First Wave of economic and social change to move across the earth, the industrial revolution triggered a second great wave of change 300 years ago. Today we are feeling the impact of the Third Wave of historic change—and it is transforming the American economy.

We are beginning to shift from a Second Wave manufacturing economy based on auto, steel, textile, apparel, and rubber to a Third Wave economy based on communications, genetics, aerospace, oceans, new materials, environmental technologies, new forms of agriculture, and an array of new services. As this shift matures, our biggest Second Wave corporations—the companies that were most successful during the industrial period—are compelled to restructure themselves.

That's why AT&T, General Motors, and many other corporations are now desperately struggling to recast themselves in a new form.

As the economy shifts, we see a new style of corporate organization. The typical Second Wave company is engaged in the mass manufacture of products and services, while the Third Wave company uses advanced technology to produce increasingly demassified—i.e., customized—products or services. Short runs are increasingly common. (Mass production, once thought to be the most advanced form of production, is now a backward form.)

The Second Wave company seeks maximum scale. It wins by brute force. The Third Wave company seeks minimum *appropriate* scale. It wins by maneuver. The Second Wave company favors vertical integration. The Third Wave company prefers to contract out, thereby retaining the high flexibility needed for success in a fast-changing environment. The Second Wave company is national; the Third Wave company is likely to be regional, local, or multinational. The Second Wave company often produces high pollution. The Third Wave company recycles and works hard to sell its by-products. The Second Wave company is usually capital intensive; the Third Wave company less so. The Second Wave company has a centralist emphasis; the Third Wave firm is more decentralist. One organization is based on permanent functions, the other on temporary functions.

In companies typical of the Second Wave, everybody reports to one boss. Everybody knows his or her foreman. In the newer, Third Wave industries, an employee may report to several bosses, each for a different project, and may, indeed, *be* the boss on yet another project.

More fundamentally, we can sum it up this way: In a Second Wave company, machines and buildings are seen as assets, while people are seen as expenses. In a Third Wave company, machines and buildings are seen as expenses, and people as assets—especially, creative people.

*   *   *

By now, the long-range characteristics of the Third Wave economy should be becoming clearer. A small, highly productive manufacturing sector, relying on very advanced production of demassified products, parallels a growing complex service sector. Both of these turn out products not for an undifferentiated mass marketplace, but for a highly segmented, continually changing market. Products are targeted and tailored for minimarkets, even individual customers. This demassification of the market parallels the growing demassification of production.

All this implies the demassification of resources as well. Instead of using a few critical resources in vast quantities, a Third Wave economy moves toward the use of multiple, more diversified resources in smaller quantities.

As the service sector grows larger, training—part of the information industry—becomes a major, in fact a basic, industry. Continuous retraining becomes one of the critical inputs to production.

The very location of work begins to shift. Work is increasingly decentralized, with some people actually working at home in "electronic cottages" and more people actually doing work for themselves, rather than for the marketplace.

As these pieces of the Third Wave economy come together, the almost total obsolescence of our conventional economic and financial tools stands revealed. "Economic science" is increasingly obsolete. The concepts, the very vocabulary we lean on, no longer provide us with adequate maps of the territory. The economic landscape is in upheaval. Our maps don't reflect it.

Recently I heard the chairman of the President's Council of Economic Advisers use the term GNP sixty-two times in forty-five minutes. His listeners—the CEOs of America's leading companies—nodded sagely as though the term still meant the same thing it did 25 years ago—as though the production of an economy based largely on services, information, and experiences could be compared with the production of material goods. I felt as though I were among medieval scholars discussing angels on the head of a pin, because the concept of GNP itself is increasingly obsolete. Designed for a mass production–mass consumption, goods-oriented economy, in which manufacturing played the dominant role, our conceptual tools simply measure the wrong things.

*   *   *

Can we handle the profound dislocations produced by the shift from a Second Wave to a Third Wave economy? We'd better.

Unfortunately, too many leaders in business and government think they can hold onto the past. These are companies, unions, and politicians who believe we must restore the Second Wave economy. They tell us to "reindustrialize," meaning that we should somehow go back to the way things were. These are people who would love to re-create the 1950s. They demand government credits, protective tariffs, even nationalization in order to accomplish that goal—anything to keep the old Second Wave industries running. They fail to see that the old basic industries will never be basic again, and the old economy based on them can never reincarnate itself.

Another group takes the opposite position—one that is, however, just as bad. They reject the bail-out approach. Let nature handle it, they say. An invisible hand will solve the crisis for us, and all those displaced workers from auto and steel or textiles will find jobs in Silicon Valley.

That is an absolute myth. Without some government intervention, without compassion, without planning, without training, millions of those workers will never be re-employed. The magic of the market cannot cure all ills. The idea that it can is based on an out-of-date picture of the labor market. It assumes that jobs are essentially interchangeable. It ignores the rise of demassification. Yet the demassification of production and distribution means that fewer jobs are interchangeable.

Not long ago, when we were shooting a television special based on my book, *The Third Wave*, we visited a foundry in the Northeast, very much like the one in which I worked for several years as a blue-collar worker. What struck me was the realization that not only were those foundry workers incapable of getting or holding a job in Silicon Valley, so were their managers. Their style is wrong. Their dress is wrong. The way they think is wrong. The way they handle authority is wrong. There is a new, Third Wave work culture, and these Second Wave people, both workers and managers, are not part of it.

The problems of unemployment, therefore, are not just economic, but cultural, and not just quantitative, but qualitative. It's not just a question of producing X million jobs, but of matching a set of changing skill requirements with a population that has to be retrained continually. It also means helping millions of people move out of the Second Wave culture into a Third Wave culture. We don't even begin to know how to do that.

For this reason, we are moving into a period that is going to test our political acumen. What is needed is fresh thinking, a recognition that the old ideologies, whether of the left or of the right, are themselves products of Second Wave culture and are therefore increasingly obsolete.

A fundamental global transformation is taking place. We are either going to manage that restructuring in a peaceful way or we are going to break ourselves up in the effort.

I therefore ask that we start doing some long-range thinking. Start thinking about the *conversion* of old industries to new products; start helping industries, unions, localities, and community organizations to undertake conversion planning. This process must be highly decentralized, and it must involve not just management, and not just finance, but also employees and even their families, along with public officials.

Finally, of course, we should nurture the new industries in optics, in lasers, bio-technology, software, video, telecommunications, and imaginative new services—especially human services, such as care for, or work with, the elderly. Above all, we must nurture new forms of education because you can't have a Third Wave economy with a Second Wave school system, which is what we now have.

Rather than fighting to preserve the past, we need to envision a future based on the new realities. The crisis we are passing through is not just American or French or German or Japanese. It is global. It is not just economic. It is social, political, and cultural, and it requires strategic thinking on all these levels. We either change intelligently or we suffer the terrifying consequences. We are—ready or not—in the process of creating a new society, a civilization of the Third Wave.

DISCUSSION

SPEAKER 1: One institution you did not mention is religion. How do you see religion reacting to this whole change process? It's such a traditional structure today. How will it be affected?

TOFFLER: I am no expert on either theology or religious organization. But if what I am saying is correct and we are moving toward increasing heterogeneity, that would suggest more diversified religious beliefs, more variety, more decentralized structures within the churches themselves. The cardinal virtue of the Third Wave must be toleration for variety, toleration for diversity. The one thing a Third Wave society cannot afford is fanaticism—the attempt to impose one view on everybody.

I would add that we all need to recognize how deep today's changes really are. They add up to a new economic base for society. Whether you call it Third Wave isn't important. After my book, *The Third Wave*, was published, some economists began talking about "sunset industries" versus "sunrise industries." Others now speak about "standardizing industries" versus "flexible industries." (These correspond to "mass" and "demassified.") But the terminology is not important. Something very big and very deep is happening.

When that happens, people are confronted by painful choices and a lot of unknowns. Any institution that can help people understand their own value systems, any institution that can help people clarify their own individual value systems instead of simply imposing a value system, can be very useful in helping them cope with change. Some religions do that well. Others, by insisting on a super-simplistic, completely black and white set of values, do not.

SPEAKER 2: Are you optimistic about the potential for retraining millions of relatively unskilled Second Wave assembly line workers whose training until now has been in repetitive work?

TOFFLER: A significant percentage of that Second Wave work force *is* retrainable, particularly the younger workers. Retraining does not just mean everybody becomes a computer programmer. Society cannot live by computers alone. For example, I believe we are going to generate a great many new service occupations. We are going to see repair services for the new technologies.

We are going to see a proliferation of highly individualized human services, like care for the elderly. In other words, many new niches are opening up for which many of those Second Wave workers *can* be retrained.

Nevertheless, we also need realism. Some workers cannot be retrained. And that means early retirement. It means some kind of public support and help. We are not going to let those people die, and we should not. We are all living off their contributions to society. Many of them are our own parents and grandparents. We need to invent new arrangements that make possible their productive participation in the society, and we haven't begun to face this issue.

Once again, I believe we'll have to invest enormous amounts in training. And before we wax *too* pessimistic about the prospects, we should bear in mind that we are now developing powerful new technologies for training. Things we couldn't do before we can now do with combinations of video discs and computers for example. That increases the percentage of people who become trainable.

I also believe that, as we move toward speech-recognition technologies, you won't necessarily need to be literate to hold a job. Literacy and intelligence are not the same. In the industrial nations, illiteracy almost automatically bars you from employment. Yet most of the great leaders in world history were illiterates. They hired slaves to do their reading for them. Today there are people in the world who can speak five intertribal languages in Central Africa and know a vast amount about the world they live in. Yet they can't read.

This need for job-related literacy may well change, however. For certain jobs, which previously required that you be literate, you now can talk to the machine and the machine talks to you. This suggests the entire relationship between literacy and the economy will change. What we have to do is to reexamine the whole educational system, the delivery system as well as the objectives of the educational process.

I am not Pollyannaish. I don't believe *everybody* can make the transition, by any means. But the more people who make that transition, the fewer we have to care for. That's why renovation of the school system and the creation of a vast training enterprise are good investments.

SPEAKER 3: In a Third Wave economy, what do you see as the role of a labor union?

TOFFLER: When I was a blue-collar worker, I of course belonged to a union. I've held five different union cards at one time or another. Later on, I actually worked for one of the trade unions. In recent years, while I have frequently been invited to lecture to business people from Tokyo and Stockholm to Wall Street, I've just received my first invitation to speak to a union. It should come as no surprise which union it is. It's the Communications Workers of America—a union largely based on the Third Wave sector of the economy.

I think this personal experience of mine merely reflects the general failure of most unions to think strategically about the future. Unions face an enormous crisis, but they've scarcely begun to face it.

I happen to believe that employees in large organizations *do* need countervailing representation. If I were still working for one of the giant auto companies, I'd certainly want some collective response to corporate decisions. But most unions grew up in the Second Wave era. They reflect that fact, and they have always been reactive.

If you look closely, you see that union organization is always a mirror image of corporate organization. The corporation organizes a certain way, and the union then parallels that. Companies go from local to national, and unions follow; companies go multinational, and the unions set up an international confederation, and so forth.

Today, not only companies, but whole industries are being restructured. And union membership in the Second Wave sector is shrinking rapidly as mass-manufacturing declines. The auto workers, the steelworkers, the machinists are all losing members rapidly. These unions were designed as Second Wave insti-tutions. Their members produce uniform goods. The unions strive for uniform-ity in wages, conditions, fringe benefits, and so forth. They are a mass insti-tution designed for a society based on centralized mass production.

But what happens when we demassify and decentralize production, as we are now beginning to do? What happens when some jobs are actually shifted into the home? The knee-jerk union response to that is, "My God, that's terrible. That's the way it was in those preindustrial cottages. It's exploitation!" That *was* the way it was at the beginning of the industrial revolution. Those sweat-shops in the home *were* dreadful. But we are not now talking about the same thing. We're talking about highly educated workers working at home, using video, computers, and telecommunications in their "electronic cottages." These are not ignorant, preindustrial serfs.

Such changes mean that if unions want to survive, they will have to adopt innovative organizational structures. They're going to have to be more like as-sociations, guilds, businesses—who knows?—even churches. They may have to take on new functions, such as training. Unions, like businesses, will have to restructure themselves.

SPEAKER 4: You often speak of the regionalization of the economy. What are some of the important ways that U.S. regions are diverging?

TOFFLER: I'll start with a small example. In publishing over the past few years, we've seen the rise of a whole series of extremely successful regional pub-lications that sprang up as national magazines died. Now you have *Texas Monthly, Atlanta, New York*, and scores of similar magazines. Such magazines have sprung up because regional advertising bases now exist for them. Regional, even local, economies can now support them, while in the past most successful magazines required a national advertising base. The fact is that today some regional econ-omies are as large as the national economy was not so many decades ago. And they can now support many forms of production that once required a national market.

Moreover, as regional economies have grown large, they've developed quite different characteristics. Just compare unemployment rates, for example, from one part of the country to another. Or look at energy use. Obviously, usage is different from region to region. The cost differentials are tremendous between, say, the Northeast and the Northwest. Compare the cost of energy, for ex-ample, in Spokane, Washington, with the cost in New York City.

I think that's also increasingly true of culture and education, both increasingly important in the Third Wave industries. And look at the political differences that divide the Northeast and the Southwest.

The part of the country that industrialized first—and thus achieved dominance in the Second Wave era—is the region in the deepest trouble as we now move into the Third Wave. It's quite clear that the problems faced by the Northeast are sharply different from those faced by the Southwest or by the South, for that matter. So are the available human, material, and intellectual resources. In my judgment, these disparities are going to become more exaggerated, rather than less.

Look outside the United States. If you go to London, you don't see much unemployment. The south of England is working pretty steadily. If you go to the north of England, you see massive unemployment. The Scots say, "We have North Sea oil, so why should we be represented by London?" You see a parallel in France, where the Bretons and Corsicans are demanding regional autonomy. You go to Belgium, and you will see written on the overpasses phrases like "pouvoir aux provinces"—power to the provinces. Quebec, western Canada, western Australia—all these regions are muttering under their breath about increased degrees of autonomy. I think that restlessness has, in large measure, an economic base.

SPEAKER 5: What is the time frame for the transition period from a Second Wave to a Third Wave economy?

TOFFLER: Nobody knows, of course. I'm thinking in terms of twenty or thirty years. We are talking about our life span. I think the transition to a Third Wave economy began in the decade from 1955 to 1965 when a number of very important changes overtook this country.

They went largely unrecognized at the time. In 1956, for the first time service and white-collar employment outnumbered blue-collar employment. In that same period you had the invention of the birth control pill, the spread of commercial jet aviation, the universalization of television, the introduction of the first business computers, the growth of conglomerates, and you had Sputnik. You had basic shifts in demography and even the arts.

Politics, economics, and social life are interrelated in ways that are not always clear. So I cannot necessarily trace all the connections, but I believe these changes helped destabilize our political system.

For example, we saw a stable political system in the United States right on through the Eisenhower years when I was a Washington correspondent and covered the White House. You could practically sleep through that administration. The changes in technology, business, demography, and culture took place at one level; the political system operated, more or less undisturbed, at another.

Then, in 1963, you got Berkeley and the assassination of John Kennedy. What followed was a decade of civil rights marches, student sit-ins, feminist consciousness raising, and political upheaval, along with a go-go economy and the landing on the moon, not to mention the Vietnam protests. And after that the political system itself began to rock and rattle.

Assassinations, the forced resignation of Nixon, two years of an unelected presidency—no one can trace all the interconnections, but I can't believe these signs of instability were wholly unrelated to the technological and social changes that began in the 1950s. I believe that American society began to feel the early buffeting of the Third Wave of change: first in technology and social life, then in politics. Now it's clear we can never go back. We are creating a new type of economy for a radically changed society.

SPEAKER 6: It appears that the Third Wave will manifest itself first in a mixed capitalistic democratic society. What does this foretell for the system of communism?

TOFFLER: The communist industrial nations face an even deeper crisis than we do. As I see it, countries are not all Second Wave or Third Wave or, for that matter, First Wave. The same country can have all three waves of change rolling through it simultaneously.

The Soviets have a very large, essentially First Wave agricultural sector—still preindustrial or partially industrialized agriculture. They have a Second Wave industrial sector. They've also got a small, essentially military Third Wave high-tech sector.

Now their problem is this. If you want a Third Wave society or a Third Wave economy, you need innovation, creativity, diversity, and dissent. You need "mind workers" rather than just "muscle workers," and for mind workers to function, you need a less authoritarian organization of work and of society. You need risk takers, not bureaucrats. You need people who question orders. In short, intellectual, cultural, and political freedom are the price of techno-logical and economic innovation. And it is a price the Soviet elite cannot af-ford to pay, except at great risk to itself. This openness, this willingness to permit error, is the precondition of the new economy. You can't have an ad-vanced Third Wave economy without it, because brains and imagination are the basic fuels of the new economy.

So, as I see it, the Soviets are caught in exactly the situation Marx himself described: Their "social relations of production" are "fettering" the further de-velopment of the "means of production." And that is Marx's exact definition of a society facing revolutionary transformation.

IV. GROWTH PROSPECTS FOR TRADITIONAL INDUSTRIES

William N. Cox, Moderator

Certainly, our growing and evolving nation has created significant growth opportunities for the emerging industries on which we have focused. But our era also has posed problems for our traditional industries, including those that have provided jobs and profits since the dawning of the Industrial Revolution.

We have witnessed the traumatic market changes that have jolted such industries as auto manufacturing. That industry has been forced to comply with a host of federally mandated environmental and safety regulations and to rescale vehicles to meet the demands of consumers faced with gasoline at $1.30 a gallon. We've seen the trials of traditional "smokestack" companies that once provided the muscle for national economic growth; today we see them cutting back on staffs and facilities as they struggle to modernize obsolescent mills in the face of foreign competition from more efficient—or unfairly subsidized—producers abroad.

In the Southeast, the textile and apparel industries have offered a graphic example of the challenges faced by traditional industries. When they built their turn-of-the-century mill towns, textile firms planted the seeds for a number of our major cities in the Piedmont region. Today we see the textile operations trying to automate their aging plants to become more efficient and competitive.

Thomas N. Roboz has been a leader in the apparel industry that provides so many jobs in both the Southeast and the Northeast. He will share his opinions on the innovations that can lead to growth in a troubled industry.

Roboz, chairman of the Charlotte-based Stanwood Corporation, is an executive whose opinions are given a lot of weight by apparel executives. He has been a leader in that industry. Just a couple of years ago, he simultaneously held three critical industry assignments: He served as either chairman or president of the American Apparel Manufacturers Association, the U.S. Apparel Council, and the International Apparel Federation.

He is uniquely qualified to serve in that international role. A native of Budapest, Hungary, he speaks five languages. His career experience includes directing a German textile firm, as well as handling more conventional domestic assignments for U.S. corporations.

Over the past few years, the U.S. government has called on Tom to serve as an adviser in its sometimes contentious trade negotiations with China to determine the volume of Chinese apparel imports that we will allow into this country.

THOMAS N. ROBOZ

Apparel: Innovations That Will Lead to Growth

In order to help you understand where our industry is going, let me re-cite a few very basic statistics to provide a benchmark.

The textile industry in 1981 reported profits as a percentage of sales after tax of 2.4 percent. In 1982 it was 1.9 percent. Profit, as a percentage of equity after tax, in the textile industry was 9.4 percent in 1981, 7.5 percent in 1982.

The apparel industry's profit on sales in 1981 was 2.9, but fell in 1982 to 1.8. Equity declined from 6.7 to 5.5.

Employment in 1973 was 2,500,000 people; in 1982, 1,900,000 people. Consumer purchases of apparel in 1973 totaled $46.5 billion. Imports in 1973 totaled 10 percent of consumption and one-eighth of production. In 1982, imports accounted for fully 25 percent of consumption and one-third of production. The percentage change of inflation from 1970 to 1982 was 1.7 percent, from 1 percent in 1981–1982. That's sobering.

The apparel industry is the largest employer of women and minorities in the United States, and in many communities in the Southeast the *only* employer. Unlike autos and steel, textiles and apparel have really remained au courant in the state of the art. We have mechanized but we have nevertheless remained strongly labor intensive. The average wage in the United States apparel industry is $4.35 an hour. In Taiwan, it's $1.45; in Haiti, it's 96 cents; in China, it's 56 cents. This is the climate in which this industry is asked to operate. Welcome to Present Shock.

The import problem has been attacked by our industry since 1960. But I want to tell you without any equivocation that any industry that relies on government protection for its future growth is eliminated by definition. It becomes noncompetitive and uninteresting to the financial community, because a single political change can make a dramatic difference.

Negotiations over textile and apparel imports are going on right now with China. I didn't even bother to go on this particular Peking venture because it was clear before we even went that nothing would happen; and nothing did. Millions of dollars' worth of goods are presently embargoed in warehouses all over the United States because of the deadlocked negotiations. There is a considerable fear that they will remain embargoed possibly until the end of this year.

Therein lies the riddle. How does an industry that is labor intensive and undercapitalized, with a miserable return on investment, leap over its own shadow? I think there's a considerable future for the apparel industry in this country but it's going to require a bloody revolution, and like most revolutions there are going to be a lot of casualties along the way.

I'm going to lay out a series of proposals as to what must happen in my industry—accomplished by ourselves, without government assistance—if we are going to have a viable apparel industry in 1990.

The first thing we must do, and we must do it rapidly, is to form multinational trading companies that will enable us to band together. With antitrust laws waived, we will be able to put together export packages. For instance, a textile shirt manufacturer could combine with a shorts manufacturer and present a tennis package. This is being done right now for Japan. This trading company must do more than export. It must start to do sourcing. There is no way out of the dilemma. The apparel companies themselves are going to have to start importing. Many already are. Most of our own branded shirt companies are among the major importers of dress shirts in the United States today. Certain lower-priced apparel is no longer economic for us to manufacture in this country.

Another thing that these trading companies must do is barter. These export product companies, formed by textile companies, must be ready, willing, and able to do that. Another thing we have to do is to become more marketing oriented. Manufacturing always has been the name of the game in American apparel and textile companies. We must get much closer to the marketplace and, indeed, we must dominate the marketplace because that is one edge we have over foreign competition.

It is interesting that I've been unable to find a capable spokesman for the retail industry to explain to my executives what is happening in retailing. I've found no volunteers. Everything in the United States is on sale right now, be it designer names, be it established brands—it's all being discounted. Department stores are complaining bitterly about losing their position in the marketplace, yet I can go into one of the top-notch department stores in Charlotte and get just as little service as I'll get at K-Mart, and very soon I'll be able to get the same merchandise at the discount store. Wrangler jeans are available at both places.

What does all this mean? It means that there's a revolution taking place in the marketplace and with the American consumer. And we've got to be extremely alert in our marketing efforts to go along with it. We also must diversify. Oxford Industries in Atlanta is one of the most successful apparel companies that has diversified. Most people forget that Lanier Business Machines was for a long time a very successful Oxford division. My company has just filed for cellular radio licenses in six markets.

Now I'm not suggesting diversification for the sake of diversification. But there are some peculiarities to the apparel industry, and one of them is cash flow. Cash flow in all apparel and textile companies peaks twice a year. We really all pay stand-by lines of credit for about nine months out of the year. We need them for three months of the year just before the big pushes, which are the back-to-school shopping season and the holiday season. Therefore, we've got to find companies that will even out our cash flow. Then we have to use our existing units for other purposes. We also have a central computing business in Knoxville, Tennessee, which has for years worked for others, that is coming out with a credit card system for selling the radio. It can do this without adding any people or more complex equipment than we have now.

We've got to find businesses that react to a different consumer impetus. The apparel and textile industries are always leading indicators of a recession and lagging indicators coming out of one. The present recession has once again proved that rule. Therefore, a different consumer impetus must be found, analyzed, and moved into.

We must also automate, as opposed to mechanizing. Mechanizing is replacing some human motion by mechanical means. Automating means eliminating humans from an operation.

MITI, the Japanese ministry of trade, feels that there is an enormous market in Europe and the United States for automated apparel plants. It is investing $66 million over three years to develop such a plant that it will sell in other nations. Robotics in the apparel industry is the most logical quick development of existing technology. We have been able to mechanize just about everything except those things that move in more than one plane.

With this particular development, the American apparel industry will be able to survive because we stand to gain a number of benefits. We no longer will be labor intensive. We will have fewer employees, more highly skilled and earning more. As far as I am concerned, those employees could make $15 an hour, it's immaterial. Average turnover is going to go down.

Today, the average turnover in an apparel plant in the United States is 5 percent per month. That means 60 percent of the labor force changes each year. It's even worse than that, because it is one-third of the labor force that is changing and it costs $3,000 to train an operator. At Stanwood, we employ 4,000 people. Just look at our training costs and how much we could afford to do if we eliminate certain of these personnel problems.

What will be the result of all of this? When we come out at the other end of the tunnel, and many of us won't, apparel companies will be much larger. They will be more specialized and much more marketing oriented. They will be a lot less flexible, but they will retain an opportunity of having small companies under their umbrellas with a maximum volume of about $20 million that will operate in the old way. They will be flexible, they will be fashion oriented, and they will be quick to respond to markets. All of this will result in a much more attractive working place, attracting much better people and, most important of all, attracting and retaining a much higher caliber of executive to the textile and apparel industry. I've had opportunities to teach at the Duke University graduate school and it's like pulling teeth to get a graduate student to go into the textile or the apparel industry.

One of the endemic problems to what I am proposing is that it requires a high degree of coordination between the fiber, textile, and apparel industries, even the retailers. And that's one thing that nobody has ever managed. But necessity is the mother of invention, and I think the situation will rapidly necessitate a great need to coordinate.

What do I mean by this? Right now, in my company, 16 percent of all piece goods received are inspected and returned as being defective for one reason or another. That has to stop. We apparel manufacturers have to be much more coordinated than we are now in sizing, in packaging; and the retailers themselves will have to get coordinated in packaging. Unless they are willing to do this, automated packaging will not work. They are moving in that direction, because they are asking us to do computerized speed ticketing, and that has to be in the same place for everyone.

I think, strangely enough, the future is very bright. We intend to be survivors. One of the greatest problems of American management is our emphasis on the quarterly report card. Some of the things that we must do will look terrible on a quarterly report but, unless we are willing to do them, we won't be around to see tomorrow. I am convinced that a highly viable American textile and apparel industry is feasible and will, indeed, be available to American industry in 1990 and thereafter.

DISCUSSION

COX: I'd like to throw out a question that's come up before: How tough will the transition be in terms of training the people?

ROBOZ: Very tough, especially in the apparel industry. This industry historically has attracted people who for various reasons could not get jobs elsewhere. For instance, they are the secondary wage earners, by and large, working for the second automobile, for the country home, or to put a child through law school.

These people really don't have too much of an opportunity. There's going to be an enormous dislocation. I well remember some years ago when we were lobbying President Carter for the industry. He said, "You don't have to convince me about the need for the apparel industry. If the Manhattan shirt factory had not been in Americus, Georgia, in bad farming times, half of those people would have starved." This is a serious moral problem, by the way. We executives are dealing with a number of constituencies: the stockholders, the suppliers, and our employees. Each one of those constituencies is vitally important, especially in a labor-intensive company. That's going to require a lot of thought, a lot of careful planning, and a lot of coordinated work by very dedicated people.

RYKE: Steve Ryke from Georgia. You mentioned that the Japanese were spending something like $60 million on this automated plant, and one of the things that you pointed out was the need to automate. Given what you said were some pretty slim profit margins, where are you going to find sources of capital to revitalize your plants?

ROBOZ: Well, if you count up the turnover costs that I cited, you will see we can achieve dramatic savings from the lower utilization of people. Furthermore, I will be quite candid in acknowledging that this program that I'm suggesting is only for the solidly capitalized textile and apparel companies. There are no rabbits in the hat and there's no magic. And it's going to call, I think, for a great deal of consolidation among the apparel and textile companies. I see a future for the small apparel company, the one with $20 million or less in revenues, because of its flexibility and its reaction to the marketplace. I see a future for the large apparel company, the firm with $75 million or more in revenues; I see no future whatever for the company in the middle. What I'm proposing is a death sentence.

GLASGOW: Merrell Glasgow from Houston, Texas. What proportion of apparel sales would you estimate will be imported ten years from now, if imports have gone from 10 to 25 percent of the U.S. market in the last ten years? What will happen in the next five or ten?

ROBOZ: I'm on record saying that by 1990 fully 50 percent of all apparel worn in this country will be imported. But I would note that a lot of that apparel will be imported by U.S. apparel companies.

LONGINO: Susie Longino, with the Atlanta Market Center. My question perhaps picks up on the flip side of the question you just answered. Could you perhaps put a dimension on the value of exports that you see with the development of export trading companies (ETCs)? Second part to the question: Are apparel manufacturers, in fact, interested in the ETC concept and, if so, to what geographic markets are they looking? You mentioned Japan as being one, but is that where the bulk of it would go, to that part of the world?

ROBOZ: As to the ETC question, we're now negotiating with three other apparel companies to form an ETC. I will be candid with you, it's like pulling teeth. First of all, the idea of combining is alien to us. We are very entrepreneurial in our industry and, too, we're all relatively inexperienced in exporting. Nevertheless, I think you are going to see this as an emerging state of the art.

As to the dollar value of exports, that ties in so much to the dollar that I am troubled to give you an honest answer. My company two years ago had exports of over $10 million. Right now we are down to $3 million. We're dealing with factors that are outside our control. Let me put it to you this way: If the dollar returns to a normal purchasing power evaluation, we will immediately be back to a $10 million export level. That would mean the industry could export as much as 18 percent of its total output. But there's a flip side to that question. Note how Hong Kong is now trading up. They are really not interested in making plain jeans any more; they are interested in making style and designer items. That's because they have a 17-percent inflation factor and their costs generally have been rising. That is not true for South Korea, however, and less true for Taiwan. It is absolutely untrue for China. They couldn't care less what a product costs as long as they get dollars for it.

V. *PRESS PERSPECTIVES*

William N. Cox, Moderator

Journalists who cover the subject of growth bring a dramatically different perspective to the subject than do the men and women in the board room. To gain the advantage of that perspective, we have asked some of the nation's top business journalists to offer their observations on growth, the corporations and industries that have achieved it, and how the press has covered the subject.

These journalists represent respected national business magazines or newspapers with national stature. They are Malcolm S. Forbes, Jr., president of Forbes; *Richard Shaffer, science and technology editor for* The Wall Street Journal; *David T. Cook, Washington economics correspondent for* The Christian Science Monitor; *and a representative from our southeastern media, James Russell, financial editor of* The Miami Herald.

Leading off our press panel will be James Russell, who covers both national and regional business for the Herald. Jim, whose weekly investment column reaches readers of about 100 newspapers around the country, will discuss the reasons behind business journalism's sudden growth.

Next will be Malcolm (Steve) Forbes, Jr., president and chief operating officer of the magazine founded by his family. Among Steve's duties is writing editorials for each issue of Forbes; *he is the third member of his family to handle that assignment. Among other things, he'll share his comments about the so-called reindustrialization of our nation.*

David T. Cook, who serves as The Christian Science Monitor's *Washington economics correspondent, will report on developments in the capital that could have an effect on corporate growth.*

Richard Shaffer will share his perspective as science and technology editor for The Wall Street Journal, *an assignment he has held since 1981. He brought to that assignment years of experience reporting on computers, medicine, and other forms of advanced technology.*

JAMES RUSSELL

When I went to school, my aim was to be a sports writer. I never expected to wind up in this field. I'm not quite sure how I got here. I learned what I learned by osmosis, by reading publications like *Forbes*, *Business Week*, *The Wall Street Journal*, and *Fortune* over the years. But I'm representing one of the real growth industries, perhaps *the* growth sector in American journalism—because business journalism or the dissemination of business information and all its facets has become a tremendous growth industry.

Forbes recognized this decades ago. It has been a great success. *The Wall Street Journal*, Dow Jones and Company, recognized it right after World War II, when it changed *The Wall Street Journal* from a narrow publication that literally went to people on Wall Street, with a circulation of about 15,000. It grew and grew. It expanded, reaching out for all the audiences that were growing as the American economy grew after the war and it now has a circulation in the neighborhood of one and a half million. That is a true growth story.

Meanwhile, the traditional American press, and I'm part of that, the daily newspaper, did not recognize all this until others had exploited it. They really stood by and did nothing for years. Now the daily press is trying to play catch-up. Newspapers are frantically expanding their business sections all over the country. They began to do this ever so slowly about eight or nine years ago, and I think the catalyst was the end of the Vietnam War. When we had the war, with all of its problems and demonstrations and divisions among the populace, that was the main story. When that ended, the number one continuing news story in the country became the economy—the economy with all its diverse elements, and diversity entered the economic scene with the advent of inflation. This was a new element that our society had not had to cope with before except on a limited basis. Most of us grew up without having to concern ourselves about inflation. Business rushed to change its ways to cope with inflation. Interest rates soared and the old 4- or 5-percent rate on savings accounts—which used to represent all the investment that most people had—that became a relic of the past. People had to make complex economic choices or get run over by the wave of inflation and high interest rates.

This forced the American public to become sophisticated in economics. Those like myself, who did not have a course in economics in college because we wanted to be sports writers, suddenly had to learn about this thing. So did every housewife, every businessman, every business executive—every individual had to learn about economics or else be run over. Countless specialized publications sprang up to feed every economic appetite.

Thousands of publications have sprung up to feed the specialized needs of business information. In general, for business information, *The Wall Street Journal* became the Bible. Everybody reads it. It has become an established American institution, and it's one that many of us have copied in our own reporting. Our own newspaper, *The Miami Herald*, finally decided about three or four years ago to strengthen our business sections. We had been forfeiting opportunities to other publications and failing to capitalize on business coverage.

Well, we did something. For one thing, we recognized the needs, and one of the needs was that *The Wall Street Journal, Forbes, Business Week*, and *Fortune* could not cover southeast Florida. We could. That was our primary circulation area.

Business there was growing by leaps and bounds. We were changing from a predominately tourist economy into a diversified economy. All kinds of businesses were entering the economy there that had never existed before, and they were largely going unreported because we simply did not have the resources to do it. And all of a sudden, playing catchup, our newspaper decided to go after it. We tripled the size of our business staff. We started a tabloid weekly insert that we call "Business Monday." Normally there's not much news in the Monday paper, but we made Monday a lively day. We cover southeast Florida thoroughly in "Business Monday."

Our management felt for a long time that there was no economic justification for increased business coverage. I thought that there was. Others did, too. And "Business Monday," which we expected to be an artistic success, also became overnight a tremendous commercial success.

Surprisingly, sixty percent of the advertising linage in "Business Monday" became what we call "plus" advertising—advertising that we were not getting before. There had been a feeling that businesses would take their ads out of other sections of the paper and put them in "Business Monday" and we would come out even. We didn't expect to gain anything commercially. It was not that way at all. We tapped an entire new market. It became a growth field for us.

Now we're being copied all around the country. We've had newspaper people from other states come down or call to consult with us about "Business Monday." They want to know how they can initiate similar sections in their own areas. The upshot is that business people are going to be watched more carefully than ever before, and I think there are good and bad aspects to that. Business is going to be reported on as never before. I think corporations are going to attract a lot of attention and will be scrutinized, but they are also going to get more publicity than ever before.

Some real professionals now are serving on newspaper business staffs. I know that, when we expanded, our management gave us the resources to hire journalists from all over the country. Other newspapers are doing this and I think this is an encouraging trend. It means American capitalism, which I consider the life support system of the free world and some of the not-so-free world, finally will get the degree of attention that it deserves in the nation's press.

MALCOLM S. FORBES, JR.

I'm very much in favor of high technology. Those of us who are learning to use word processors find them absolutely fantastic. I don't know how you measure productivity, but those word processors coming from the microprocessor have increased productivity enormously. They are doing to the typewriter what the typewriter once did to the quill, to the fountain pen, to the pencil. It is increasing enormously our ability to write, to edit. Our own editor, who is a man in his early sixties, thought he would resist the word processor when we started to put them into the office. Now he loves it. It is a great toy. Our writers don't like it so much, because now the editor can edit more than ever; he is a terror to the staff. We were growing rapidly in recent years and they thought the bigger *Forbes* got, the less hand the editor could have. They no longer think that way. The power of the boss has increased. He has more means with which to meddle in everyone's business.

We at *Forbes* magazine like to concentrate on people running companies. We like to see how the top people react and make a difference for the success or failure of a company. In these times, the technological changes taking place are providing us a lot of grist for stories. There probably hasn't been a time since the 1930s and 1940s when American business has been under as much stress and faced with as much competition as it is today.

Microprocessors, microbiology, lasers, all the high tech words you hear about, all are bringing about an enormous change. They are changing the way we use labor, the way we use capital, the way we use materials. Instead of using copper in communications, we now use fiber-optics. Instead of using as much steel as we did, we use ceramics, we use other metals, we use plastics. We're using robotics in the factories.

It wasn't the dreadnaught or the big tank that won the wars in Lebanon or the Falkland Islands in 1982. It was electronics. Electronics allowed the Israelis to shoot down eighty-three Russian planes without losing one of their own. It allowed them to destroy sophisticated Russian missiles. One Exocet missile sank a major ship in the Falklands. The microprocessor, the so-called computer on the chip, is going to do to manufacturing what manufacturing did to agriculture sixty or seventy years ago. It once took 20 to 25 million farmers to provide food for this country. Today two and a half million farmers are producing three times as much as those 25 million farmers did 50 to 65 years ago. Manufacturing is not going to disappear. The smokestacks are. We are going to be doing manufacturing differently. What we are seeing is an expansion of what Adam Smith referred to 200 years ago: an expansion of the division of labor. The division of labor makes it possible for new professions, new jobs, and new industries to arise.

It's fun to speculate on what kind of new industries, what kind of new professions, are going to pop up in the 1980s and 1990s from these extraordinary technological advances. But it would be just that, speculation. It would be fun but it would also be rather foolish.

We are going to be surprised. For instance, take the microprocessor and the computer. Who would have dreamed a mere five or six or seven years ago that one of the great offshoots of the computer revolution would be the change in the way we play games? Atari and Pacman sound frivolous, but no one would have foreseen that they would create a billion-dollar industry. Who could have foreseen in 1910 that what Henry Ford was doing with the assembly line would change the whole way of American life?

Speculating into the future can make you look pretty foolish and silly sometimes. After World War II, a lot of prognosticators and futurists were saying that everyone was going to have an airplane or a helicopter the way most people had automobiles. It never happened. The Cessnas never became the GMs of the American economy. So you can speculate but that's all you can do. There are going to be surprises. Most ideas won't work but the ones that do will jolt us and change the way we do things, the way we see things.

In our own sphere at *Forbes* magazine, we look at things in three arbitrary classifications.

You might call the first category myths, legends, or just sheer misperceptions. There are a number of legends and myths that color the way many reporters cover the economy.

You hear, for instance, that the service economy simply means a lot of low-skill, minimum-wage fast food jobs—that it really boils down to our doing each other's laundry. That's how the trade unionists denigrate what is happening in the economy today, doing each other's laundry. They are right to an extent. They have indeed touched upon what economics is all about. It's exchanging goods and services. If you do my laundry, I might give you in exchange a copy of *Forbes* magazine or, more enticingly, a ride in a balloon. That's what economic activity is all about—it's exchange. We are not going to be silly enough to do each other's laundry. There's no benefit in that. Through the medium of money, we do exchange our specialties, our own goods for others' goods and services, and that is what economics is all about. We will be exchanging goods and services, however, in ways that we haven't done before.

Another myth is that high tech will be the death of manufacturing. It won't be. It will change the way we manufacture but we're still going to be a manufacturing economy. We're still going to have a strong manufacturing base, just as a shrinking number of people in agriculture didn't mean that we ceased to be an agricultural power. High tech just means that fewer people are going to be able to do far, far more than we ever thought possible in the past.

Let me give you another example—railroads. Thirty-five years ago in this country railroads employed two and a half million people. Today they employ 350,000 people and are carrying much more freight than those two and a half million did years ago. On the other hand, the computer industry employed only a few thousand people thirty-five years ago. If you take it all today, salesmen, merchandisers, manufacturers, the whole scope of the computer industry and its offshoots, you are probably talking about two and a half to three million people.

The economy is always changing. The changes may go through periods of acceleration, such as we have today. But most of the time, if we have prosperity, we don't notice the changes very much. When you go into an economic crisis such as we had in the 1970s, these changes are suddenly magnified. They suddenly become politicized. So that's another myth. We are not going to see the death of manufacturing.

Another myth that we reporters often hear is that services and high tech are parasites on true manufacturing. Just look at this past recession. Manufacturing really got hit hard. Where did employment hold its own and increase? In the so-called service sector. That shows the underlying strength of the kind of changes I am talking about.

Just look at the so-called information industry. People say information for what? That's like asking what steel is used for. Steel is used for railroads, for skyscrapers, for cars. What is this information society going to be used for? It's a means to an end. We see retailers being able to get more up-to-date information on inventories. People certainly know the impact it's had on banking and on insurance. It's a means to an end. It's a form of a raw material.

Services finally are not homogeneous. That is another myth. When you say service sector, you are lumping a whole bunch of things together. Just start to break it down. Utilities are classified as a service— the providing of electricity—and obviously are very capital intensive.

Communications and fast foods, by contrast, are not capital intensive but very labor intensive. In tax preparation, you don't need much capital or much labor. All you need is somebody who can pretend to have familiarity with the tax code. Just keep in mind when you talk about services that it covers a whole array of things.

Moreover, the distinction that so many of us try to make between manufacturing and services is a false one. They are closely intertwined. Take, for example, the automobile. A car is a manufactured product, yet it can be used as a service. The same with trucks: One leads to the other. What makes it possible to sell an automobile? It's a financial service—providing a customer credit to buy a car. If you want to sell a product overseas, you need to ship it. That's a service. You need to insure it. That's a service. They are intertwined. One feeds the other. One stimulates the other. You can't have one without the other.

The division is an arbitrary one. It was devised by the economists to analyze the economy, but it often isn't very good in terms of coming up with the proper policies that would most benefit the economy. So that's one area that you might call myths and legends. There are a lot of them and they color the way we cover the economy.

My second general category is the reaction of our political leadership to these extraordinary changes. Change does not take place in a vacuum. It can generate excitement but it can also generate fear. And this reaction by our political leadership will determine whether we will benefit fully from the changes that are coming up or whether we are going to thwart them and not get the full benefit from them.

When we went to school, we learned the agrarian myth about the sturdy farmer being the backbone of the nation. How do we keep the farmer on the farm? How do we preserve the farmer? These myths color our political actions. For the most part, they are harmless. All we did was give price subsidies to the farmer. We didn't save him. We just made the rich ones richer. But it can have a very damaging impact, as happened in the 1920s. The farmer was very efficient. The tractor was opening up new lands for cultivation and the farmer was producing too much. We didn't need as many farmers. So what did the farmers do? They trouped to Washington and asked for protection from what they thought was the villain of foreign competition: Washington responded, but unfortunately that political process led to a bill called the Smoot-Hawley tariff law of 1930, which set off a devastating global trade war and turned a minor American recession into a global depression. So these seemingly harmless myths that we were taught can have severe political repercussions.

We are hearing a lot these days from our politicians, such as John Glenn and Walter Mondale, about the need to reindustrialize, about the need to preserve, as John Glenn puts it, the backbone of industrial America. Baloney! I never thought it would happen, but we are beginning to turn the blue collar worker into a legend. Look at a recent issue of *Newsweek*. It's hard to believe that same magazine twelve years ago was talking about the inhumanity of working conditions in factories, about the inhumanity of the assembly line. Now we are replacing those assembly lines with robotics, creating new jobs for millions of people, and yet *Newsweek* is deploring the passing of smokestack America and the passing of the assembly line.

If we resort to protectionism, trying to turn back the clock, the economic and political repercussions could be very dangerous. After World War II, we made possible the great boom of the 1950s and 1960s because we liberalized trade laws. We repealed the Smoot-Hawley kind of thinking. We also had a sensible monetary system. Today we have anarchy in this monetary system. We're seeing an enormous increase in protectionist pressures. If we don't get liberalized trade laws in the so-called services area, we will be allowing countries to interfere with the flow of information, computer programming, and technology. Then we are going to have the kind of arthritis, a thwarting of economic progress, that we saw in the late 1920s and early 1930s.

The political leadership question will determine whether we have the atmosphere where we can harvest the real bounty of these changes that seem to be in the offing. Will our politicians be Luddites or will they be more enlightened?

The high-tech fad exists in politics in another fashion. You see it on the state and local levels. Almost every state in the union now says, "Gee, how can we bring Silicon Valley to Hoboken, New Jersey? How can we bring Boston's Route 128 to Dubuque, Iowa?" I've got an answer for them. They don't need to. Just as you didn't need a steel mill in every town to participate in the industrial revolution, so, too, you don't need Silicon Valley in every state to participate in high tech.

Seventy-five years ago, Detroit didn't try to recreate Pittsburgh. They found a very productive use for the steel that Pittsburgh and Birmingham, Alabama, were turning out. It's the same thing with technology. It is the use to which you put the technology that counts. Don't try to recreate Route 128 in your hometown. If you have the right environment, you will attract industries and entrepreneurs who will make use of this high technology just as you once found industrialists making use of raw materials like steel.

Finally, there's a favorite area of mine and that is Wall Street, the boom in new stock issues. If you have a high-tech sounding name, you can become a millionaire. It doesn't matter what you do. Just have the right name and Wall Street can sell it today. It's going to provide journalists with a lot of good stories. Beware of this hype; when your broker calls you—watch out. The brokers are going to be the ones who make the money.

Finally, our third category is how well our hard-hit manufacturing sector responds to these great changes. They can find inspiration in the past from people like Henry Ford and Ray Kroc, if they realize that the absence of the smokestack does not mean the absence of manufacturing.

What did Henry Ford teach us? He taught us that you could produce things for less money. That is the key: producing things for less money. Make them cheaper. Whether you produce them in great quantity or little quantity, make them cheaper. If you make them cheaper, as we see with microprocessors, you find new uses for them, even frivolous things like Atari games.

One hang-up that manufacturers have in this country is the notion that their primary cost is labor. It isn't. And this is where Henry Ford comes in. He showed that you could make products cheaper and yet pay your workers twice the prevailing wage of industrial America at that time. That is what the Japanese do. You look at the difference between the cost of a Japanese car and that of an American car. It is roughly $2,000. Only about $600 of that is labor. The rest is better manufacturing techniques. Henry Ford showed how you could produce things for less and pay your workers more.

What do hamburgers have to do with reindustrialization or high technology? They have a lot to do with it. What Ray Kroc did with hamburgers is what we should be doing with more of the service sector. He used manufacturing techniques and controls to turn what was a high-cost, low-profit industry into one that made a lot of money, one that grew enormously to meet people's needs. It may seem simple today, because we now take fast foods for granted, but it was a revolution when he started in the 1950s. When people say in the service sector "how do you get productivity or how can a barber cut more hair?", you just look at what Ray Kroc did with the restaurant industry. Use your imagination. I think you can find enormous applications in other service industries as well.

This high-tech stuff really does open up awesome possibilities and opportunities for the American economy. It really does allow us an opportunity to end play the Germans and the Japanese and all the nemeses of the late 1960s and 1970s. Creativity and imagination are the keys. Committees and bureaucracies are not conducive to creativity. Individualism is.

In the years ahead, instead of reading books about Theory Z management or how Samurai swords can be used to get more productivity from your workers, you'll start seeing books once again on a thing called Yankee ingenuity.

Finally, one last observation. What seems dazzling now when you talk about lasers, microprocessors, or genetics may seem mundane ten or fifteen years down the road. We'll take them for granted and something else will excite us. Just go back to the late nineteenth century to the railroads. When they were being built, poems were written about them. Lyrics were written about the wonderful railroads. What happened when the railroads came in? Farmers started to complain about the prices the railroads charged. People thought of them as big robber barons plundering the countryside. I don't know what the equivalent will be with high tech, but I can guarantee it will come and we journalists will be there to write about it.

DAVID T. COOK

Official Washington may be oblivious to much of what passes for reality among those of us whose joy it is to fund congressional spending. But the inhabitants of the City of Smoke and Mirrors are not oblivious to the fact that fundamental changes are taking place in the nation's industrial structure as Rust Bowl industries desperately try to slim down at the same time the typical 20-year-old software designer is driving off into the sunset in a Porsche.

Like journalists, our national legislators seem to get secret pleasure from continually rediscovering and then announcing that the sky is falling. But one does not have to be prone to hysteria to see that the Japanese are trying to do to the computer and aerospace industries, among others, what they have already done to autos and consumer electronics. In 1980, 50 percent of the U.S. trade surplus in high technology flowed from two targeted industries—computers and aerospace.

Meanwhile, recent studies on the effectiveness of Japanese targeting of the machine tool and semiconductor industries have helped make industrial policy almost as popular a topic of conversation in Washington as the subject of which of the President's aides will be promised Mr. Reagan's undying support and then will resign the next day.

Industrial policy is subject to a host of definitions, depending upon your ideological stripes. The core of such policy is nurturing the fastest possible economic growth. Republicans generally favor an approach of modified economic Darwinism where the sick are left to die and the healthy allowed to thrive—as long as the sick aren't bumped off by government regulation or burdensome taxes. Democrats tend to favor intensive care for terminally ill industries and an extra ration of fiscal growth hormones for healthy firms.

It is not surprising that every other congressman has suddenly become an industrial physician. As Robert J. Samuelson wrote in a recent issue of the *National Journal*, "Industrial policy comes down to people.

Will there be jobs for them?" That brings the issue down to the gut political level.

An unpublished Cabinet Council study provides clear evidence of the important role high tech plays in our economy. Unpublished Washington reports are documents leaked to any reporter with a remote interest in the subject. That October 1982 study found that high-tech growth firms:

One—had a growth rate twice that of the economy as a whole. Nine of the ten fastest growing industries in recent years have been in the high-tech field. Two—enjoyed labor productivity growth six times as fast as the overall business population. Three—showed price increases during the 1970–1980 period only one-third as high as the country's overall inflation rate.

Finally, since 1975, high-tech firms have produced a cumulative surplus in the balance of trade of $128 billion compared to the nation's cumulative $148 billion deficit in total merchandise trade during the same period. So even in the play money land of Congress, we are talking high stakes.

Of course, we already have an industrial policy of sorts aimed at growth, among other goals. According to that dispassionate observer of the economic scene, Senator Gary Hart, Democrat of Colorado, corporate America in 1980 fed at the federal trough to the tune of $304 billion in industrial assistance through direct outlays and tax expenditures. A tax expenditure is money the government could have taxed away from you but decided not to through the goodness of its heart.

Any time you spend that much money, there are a few anomalies. In 1980, for example, Uncle Sam made $455 million available in tax breaks for the timber industry but nothing in direct aid to semiconductor producers. At the same time, the government spent five times more on research and development for commercial fisheries than on research into new steel technology.

But the government's industrial policy efforts extend beyond the aquatic arena. Defense Secretary Caspar Weinberger and his cohorts play an important role in certain emerging growth areas. For example, the Pentagon is sponsoring development of new techniques for forging super alloys and producing composite materials. The Air Force and NASA are spending $75 million to develop an automated factory of the future.

Whatever the long-term effects of such spending, the Reagan Administration is proposing a significant increase in R&D spending. It has asked for $45.8 billion in R&D obligation authority for fiscal year 1984, with $30 billion of that going to defense. The defense share is up $6.7 billion while civilian research would climb $220 million. Of course, these totals are the administration's wish list with changes sure to be made by Congress.

You don't have to make cruise missiles to profit from some recent federal action to promote growth. Last year Congress passed a 25-percent tax credit for incremental R&D spending. But even Bruce Merrifield, assistant secretary of commerce for productivity and technology, says the tax credits have been "totally useless" in encouraging investment in R&D.

Treasury regulations were cleverly drawn so that only firms already selling products could qualify for the credit. Those not yet offering a product to the market were shut out. So an estimated 95 percent of the $2 billion in credits went to struggling enterprises like IBM, which otherwise would have had to mortgage the family home in Armonk, New York to come up with the research funds.

Commerce Secretary Malcolm Baldrige admitted recently to Congress that "there may be a need to extend the scope of the existing 25 percent tax credit." He added that the administration is "looking into" changing this and other tax law provisions.

From the "imitation is the sincerest form of flattery file" comes another administration measure designed to spur growth. Earlier this year the Commerce Department started an industrial technology partnership program paralleling the Japanese in some respects. The program allows large firms to join together in a consortium to research, develop, and produce expensive high-tech products. A group of electronics firms are working in such a consortium, and legislation has been introduced by representative Ed Zschau, Republican of California, to permanently authorize such joint research and permit development projects.

While industrial policy is the subject of a lot of talk on Capitol Hill, don't expect too much in the way of precedent-shattering action during this session. As you know, Congress has a few other things on its mind, including budget deficits, defense spending, domestic content legislation, and the 1984 elections. But some action from Washington aimed at boosting growth is possible.

First, the likely unilateral action: The White House reportedly is considering naming a panel of corporate executives who would propose ways of bolstering high-tech business. And Commerce official Merrifield says the administration is working on possible revisions in the antitrust laws that would put U.S. firms on a more equal footing with their industrial competitors in Japan when it comes to working together to save a dying industry and being able to sell excess capacity to a competitor.

Merrifield argues that "you can make a pretty good case that the antitrust laws are really irrelevant now simply because the technology is moving so rapidly that new technology supersedes the old well before the useful life of a product can be reached."

We may also see action from Congress on growth-related items with bipartisan appeal. The House has passed legislation to spend $400 million beefing up high school mathematics and science education. Hearings on a similar measure have been held in the Senate.

Fatter budgets for basic research are also a fairly popular item on Capitol Hill. The administration is proposing an increase of $300 million, to $1.9 billion in federal support, for general science and basic research at the National Science Foundation and Department of Energy.

Finally, there is considerable bipartisan support for rule changes that would make it easier for growth firms to tap pension funds as a source of capital. Current rules, some imposed at the state level, require pension trustees to invest only in companies that meet stringent standards on value of stock outstanding and dividend payment record.

As important as what Congress does this year is what it decides not to do. What you are not going to get is everyone's favorite strawman, a government agency on the Japanese model that would select winners and losers. Republicans object to such a plan on ideological grounds. The latest report of the President's Council of Economic Advisers notes matter-of-factly that, as the economy becomes more specialized, "some sectors will grow and others will shrink. . . . Prices and wages in some U.S. heavy industries are probably too high to be sustainable in an integrated world economy." Take that, Detroit and Pittsburgh.

In the Republicans' view, the government's role is to "remove barriers and create a conducive environment," says Commerce Secretary Baldrige. "The targeting role belongs to entrepreneurs and to the rest of the private sector." The Democrats would do more to help prop up ailing firms and spur new ones but most of them reject targeting, at least partly because of the political problems involved in selecting the economic sectors or geographic regions to be bolstered or euthanized.

Key staff aides to Democratic leaders in the House and Senate have been meeting recently, working out details of an industrial recovery package. To date, no consensus has been reached. Last year's House Democratic Caucus report on "Long-Term Economic Policy" does provide some idea of where the party is going. "We must make our basic industries competitive again. That will require broad-based investment," it stated.

Meanwhile, Senate Democrats like John Glenn of Ohio have weighed in with suggestions for a science and technology department while Gary Hart wants the President to help negotiate long-term agreements among labor, management, and government to make industry more competitive. We will hear much more of this in the upcoming presidential campaign. Those with a low tolerance for demagoguery, beware.

RICHARD SHAFFER

In writing my weekly column for *The Wall Street Journal*, I use computers a lot. I usually write about twice as much as I need and having the computer helps me trim, and probably increases the chances that the best of what I write makes it into the paper. At present there are five computer systems in my home and office.

In addition, however, I often find myself resorting to the old ways—writing under pressure, just ahead of deadline, on a manual typewriter. It's my job to explain the frontiers of technology and to forecast its changes as they affect business. But I often do so on a plain old typewriter, a machine invented in 1873. Why? Because sometimes a typewriter is the best tool for the job. I also prefer paper and pencil for organizing my thoughts. I subscribe to several data-base services, but it's often easier and faster to find out what I want to know in an ordinary library. Sometimes, for even faster service, I ask an expert. I own and have used income tax programs, but an accountant usually does my taxes. It's really easier that way.

On the whole, I have found very few applications in which a computer really does for me what I need most: Save time. These personal experiences have made me more than a little skeptical about most of the forecasts for the growth industry of tomorrow. As a boy, I used to read a lot of similar forecasts in magazines called Popular This and Popular That and Scientific Whatever. Computers were going to run your home tomorrow and a computer was going to be on every manager's desk soon. Most of those forecasts have turned out to be about as accurate as the ads in the back of those magazines that told me I could make big money in my spare time sharpening saws.

With that caveat, let me look at some economic history and offer some forecasts of my own. Industries founded in the nineteenth century and earlier—petroleum refining, metal, and food processing—still dominate our manufacturing. Yet the twentieth-century computer industry has become so economically significant that more money was spent in 1981 to buy mainframe and minicomputers and related products than on aircraft and aircraft services—about $30 billion. Car making remains America's largest manufacturing industry. But in the last decade, computer shipments have risen to a level of 40 percent of passenger car sales (from 20 percent in the early 1970s). At the same time, the price of cars has doubled and the price of computing power has declined by 90 percent.

Electronic parts now surpass aluminum in economic significance if the value of annual shipments is any measure. Telephone equipment and services account for more of the Gross National Product than steel. Some of these large new industries are also rapidly growing, and the growth is expected to continue. The government's most recent Industrial Outlook identified ten industries that are likely to grow at real rates of 8 to 10 percent in each of the next five years. That's the fastest pace in the economy. They range from electronic computers and plastics to analytical instruments and telecommunications equipment.

The computer forecast is hardly surprising. The machines are almost everywhere. They are in accounting departments and in military and research organizations. Small computers are appearing on desk tops and disappearing into ovens, watches, typewriters, and video games. So many tiny computers are working under the hood of today's automobile to increase mileage and lower pollution that a single car maker, General Motors, actually manufactures more computers, albeit smaller ones, every year than International Business Machines Corp. and all other computer system manufacturers combined.

If the computer trend continues, and I think it will, it should brighten the outlook for related industries. For example, the prospects for the computer services business should be excellent. That business has survived several shakeouts. A few substantial companies have emerged and dozens more are showing rapid growth and high profits. Computer software looks good, too. About $20 billion is spent annually on software. Yet the potential remains large even for automating such earthly chores as the processing of inventory and purchasing records. Even today, half of all manufacturing companies still handle those tasks manually, with file cards.

Computers now help design products ranging from switching engines to electronic switches. Indeed, it is no longer possible to design a new computer or even most computer parts without the aid of a computer. The human mind, or even several human minds working together, cannot deal with such complexity and detail. That bodes well for the field of computer-aided design.

Microprocessors may soon mimic human thought well enough that relatively inexpensive desk-top computers can automatically diagnose many diseases, prepare income tax returns, give investment advice, solve algebra and calculus problems. Thus, a boom is likely in the field known as artificial intelligence.

Let's look at communications. Gutenberg spent five years setting the Bible in type. Today, the book can be transmitted in electronic form over ordinary copper telephone lines in less than an hour. The Bible however, can be sent in less than a second through optical fibers, the clear glass threads that transmit information as flashes of light instead of pulses of electricity. With information-carrying powers of that magnitude, it's not surprising that optical fibers are expected to be one of the highest growth industries.

Deregulation and the breaking up of American Telephone & Telegraph Co. offer plenty of opportunities for manufacturing telephone equipment. More obscure fields are promising, too. One involves the integrated power circuit, a little switch that can handle high voltages and currents instead of the mere trickle of electricity common in microelectronics today. Demand for high-voltage integrated circuits in a few years could amount to $1 billion annually. The semiconductor industry even seems to be looking up again. Custom and semicustom integrated circuits may be a promising avenue to profits. In addition, some technologies that have been around quite a while are suddenly looking more promising. One is CMOS, a way of making integrated circuits that use very little electric power. Flexible manufacturing may bring a new era in which it's economical to make one-of-a-kind products.

Overall, advanced technology may create millions of new jobs in this decade. But advanced technology industries are changing as they grow and the changes could have a profound effect on the mix of new jobs and their geographic distribution. Before the end of the decade, microcomputers undoubtedly will displace mainframes as the largest segment of the computer industry, just as automobiles surpassed trains as the biggest transportation sector just after the turn of the century. That transition will fundamentally alter the nature of computer manufacturing, marketing, distribution, service, and software.

Look what's happening already. A decade ago, in the age of minicomputers, most were manufactured in Massachusetts. Now, with home computers and personal computers you might expect that most of them come from California. But the number one state is probably Texas, where Apple, Tandy, and Texas Instruments have factories. Alabama may even rank high, too, because of all the IBM personal computer work done in Huntsville. As these desk-top computers proliferate—there are 150 brands now—technology is beginning to take a back seat to marketing skills, financial resources, and distribution ability. Only a few years ago, any company that could build a microcomputer could sell it, and most of them seemed to. Today, many newcomers are finding the going very, very rough.

It also is possible to argue that the semiconductor industry had reached a stage where manufacturing skill has become more important to profits than inventiveness so that a mere clever circuit design innovation no longer will guarantee rapid growth as in the past. Thus, the semiconductor industry also could become even more the domain of larger companies.

Corporate heavyweights such as Bendix, General Motors, and General Electric have entered the robot market, joining an already impressive list of competitors from abroad. Can the industry possibly support the five dozen companies now making robots? Perhaps.

Look at the history of computing. When electronic digital computers first became commercial just after World War II, forecasters predicted that no more than a dozen machines ever would be needed. IBM even decided not to sell computers because the market seemed too small. Yet at some point in the very near future, the computers on our planet probably will outnumber the people.

But forecasts are wrong in the other direction, too. Remember aerospace engineering, nuclear power, plastics, environmental science, geology? All of those were growth occupations not too long ago. Tried looking for work as an environmental scientist or a petroleum reservoir engineer lately? High tech is subject to the same laws of economics as everything else, as well as to those of physics and biology. Emerging technologies have to compete with older ways of doing the same things, which are sometimes cheaper and usually far better understood by the customer.

In the present economic slump, growth industries are having their troubles, too. Computers, for example, have not been immune to recession, contrary to popular industry belief. Maybe robots one day will put thousands of workers on the streets. Maybe they also will create new opportunities for blue-collar workers to build and repair robots but, at the moment, most robot companies have attracted a lot more publicity than orders. The apparent upsurge in robot sales has come largely from the number of companies entering the business. Many companies are selling robots, but only a few of them, which hardly constitutes a boom for the manufacturers. Eventually these technologies will become an even more fundamental part of our economy, but as computers and semiconductors and robots become more important to the economy, the economy will become more important to them.

As high technology penetrates an increasing number of economic sectors—for example, consumer goods, small business, and housing—high-technology industries become more cyclical, too. Moreover, the siren song of high technology has brought virtually every state into competition for its share of a field that cannot possibly support them all. A few years ago economic developers in most states tried to ride the gradual transition of the U.S. economy from a manufacturing to a service base. They tried to attract insurance, distribution, and finance companies. Then they began to see that we can't all sell each other insurance, or shine each other's shoes. Somebody has to make something. Somebody has to sell it. When shopping malls were hot, every city built one. Most cities built dozens. Now, who is making money in shopping centers?

In the same way, we are rushing into high technology as some sort of salvation, and it too will be disappointing for most of us. We are praising high-technology managers and damning those in smokestack industries. But I've been in the news business long enough to understand something about cycles, and the time will surely come when we discover that high-tech managers are only human, too, and even they have let us down.

In short, I'm not the most optimistic person you could find about high-tech growth industries. Whenever I hear about how the world will be new or more promising just the day after tomorrow, well, I'm a newspaper man and I'm a professional skeptic—instead of saying, "Golly, Mr. Wizard, ain't science grand?" I usually say, "Oh, really?"

Growth Industries in the 1980s: Conference Registration

Andrews, Dan, First National Bank of Dickson, Tennessee
Auletta, Patrick V., Society Corporation
Avery, David, Federal Reserve Bank of Atlanta
Bachman, John W., Edward D. Jones & Co.
Bahary, Emil S., American Bell
Ball, Charles E., The First National Bank of Boston
Banton, Julian W., Southtrust Bank of Alabama N.A.
Barker, William R., The Gates Rubber Co.
Battin, Peter C., Marba Inc.
Baty, Jerry T., Smith, Barney, Harris & Upman
Bedwell, Don, Federal Reserve Bank of Atlanta
Bell, Ron H., Astrop Advisory Corporation
Betteker, Robert L., Lighthouse National Bank
Bingham, May, Federal Reserve Bank of Atlanta
Blair, David J., White River Capital Corporation
Booker, Paulette, Federal Reserve Bank of Atlanta
Bosch, Mary P., Georgia Power Company
Botifoll, Luis J., Republic National Bank of Miami
Bowen, Stephen, Jr., Bowen Construction Company
Bradfield, Betty, Federal Reserve Bank of Atlanta
Brinson, Edward L., The Calibre Companies Inc.
Brown, Charles B., Coopers & Lybrand
Brown, Homer, First National Bank of Dickson, Tennessee
Burkhalter, Henry M., Burkhalter & Co.
Burnette, Wayne H., Alexander City Bank
Carefoot, George H., Flagship Peoples Bank of Tallahassee

Carter, Charlie, Federal Reserve Bank of Atlanta
Carter, Frank, Carter & Associates
Casey, Louie C., Jr., Flagship Bank of Jacksonville
Chapman, Don L., North by Northwest
Cheek, Tom, Vintage Enterprises Inc.
Cheng, Dinah Lin, Union Carbide Corporation
Chronopoulos, Bill, Federal Reserve Bank of Atlanta
Clawson, C. Joseph, Glendale Federal S&L Association
Coker, D. Gerald, Ford & Harrison
Colaw, Larry W., Industrial Development Staff
Collins, Tom G., Jr., Equifax
Coltrane, Donald R., First American Bank of Cleveland N.A.
Cooper, Frederick E., Flowers Industries Inc.
Cox, Bill, Federal Reserve Bank of Atlanta
Cragoe, John H., White River Capital Corporation
Davis, Gordon R., Jr., Industrial Development Council
Davis, Sandra, Federal Reserve Bank of Atlanta
Del Guercio, Michael T., U.S. Postal Service
Delvalle, Kenneth T., Campbell Soup Company
Devlin, Charles F., National Steel Corporation
Dickerson, Willard D., The First National Bank of Boston
Doyle, Joe, Federal Reserve Bank of Atlanta
Duke, R. A., Jr., American National Bank & Trust Co.
Edwards, Randy, Blue Cross of Georgia/Columbus Inc.
Ekman, A. L., First Florida Banks
Farrior, Linda, Federal Reserve Bank of Atlanta
Feinberg, Robert S., House Banking Committee
Ferguson, Thomas C., Flagler National Bank of the Palm Beaches
Fields, Dail, MCI Telecommunications Corp.
Fitzgerald, John, Holiday Inns Inc.
Fodor, Gary, Robinson Humphreys
Fox, Ned L., Lilly Industrial Coatings Inc.
Franta, Laura L., E. I. du Pont de Nemours & Co. Inc.
Frisbee, Pam, Federal Reserve Bank of Atlanta
Galloway, John, Blue Cross of Georgia/Columbus Inc.
Gates, Timothy J., Superior Linen & Apparel Services Inc.
Gatlin, Charles R., Forward Macon Inc.
Ginden, Charles B., Peachtree Bank

Glasgow, W. Merrill, Anderson, Clayton & Co.
Goff, Ronald W., Allen C. Ewing & Co.
Gomez, Jose L., Alexander Grant & Co.
Gonzalez Blanco, Roberto, Republic National Bank of Miami
Gore, Jerry, Vinings Chemical Company
Goudreau, Bob, Federal Reserve Bank of Atlanta
Graham, Douglas A., R. J. Reynolds Development Corporation
Granade, Hugh R., Tennessee Valley Authority
Gregory, Robert L., Edward D. Jones & Co.
Guthman, Sig, AECO Products Div.
Guy, Charles E., U.S. Postal Service
Haddrill, Richard, Ernst & Whinney
Hagen, John G., Eaton Corporation
Halford, Travis E., Equifax Inc.
Hancock, Fred H., The National Bank of Fitzgerald
Hanks, David W., Chart House Inc.
Harris, Wayne, Blue Cross of Georgia/Columbus Inc.
Harris, Willard B., Tultex Corporation
Haulk, Jake, Mellon Bank
Haywood, Charles, Federal Reserve Bank of Atlanta
Healy, Leigh Watson, Federal Reserve Bank of Atlanta
Hebel, Thomas A., Flagship Bank of Okeechobee
Hedrick, David E., Central Bank of Volusia County
Hewell, James R., Peachtree Doors Inc.
Hill, Bruce, Federal Reserve Bank of Atlanta
Hontzas, Thomas M., Deposit Guaranty National Bank
Hunnicutt, Don, Graphic Industries Inc.
Jennings, C. B., Jr., Peachtree Doors
Johnson, Douglas W., Ernst & Whinney
Johnson, Joan, Blue Cross of Georgia/Columbus Inc.
Johnston, Frank, First United Corp.
Jones, G. William, APAC Inc.
Juneau, Jerry, Blue Cross of Georgia/Columbus Inc.
Kahley, Bill, Federal Reserve Bank of Atlanta
Keleher, Bob, Federal Reserve Bank of Atlanta
Kelly, Joseph E., C&S Georgia Corporation
Kester, Victor P., Mayer Electric Supply Company
King, Frank, Federal Reserve Bank of Atlanta

Kline, Duane, Federal Reserve Bank of Atlanta
Koch, Don, Federal Reserve Bank of Atlanta
Kroon, George E., First Interstate Bank
Lange, Kennedy E., Georgia Power Company
Larson, L. D., Mobil
Lieberman, William J., Savannah Bank and Trust Co.
Lombardi, Paul F., Sands & Company Inc.
Longino, Susie, Atlanta Market Center
Lott, Michael H., C&S National Bank
Loudermilk, R. Charles, Aaron Rents Inc.
McAuley, Robert E., Economic Development Council/Chattanooga Area
Chamber of Commerce
McCall, Henry, Financial Institution Services Inc.
McCrackin, Bobbie, Federal Reserve Bank of Atlanta
McDonald, Michael, Federal Reserve Bank of Atlanta
McGill, Patty, Federal Reserve Bank of Atlanta
Maclellan, Hugh O., Jr., Provident Life
McRae, Walter A., Jr., Scott-McRae Automotive Group Inc.
Mahoney, James A., First National Bank of Boston
Manning, William S., The Bibb Company
Marks, Francis A., Executive Presentation Systems Corp.
Mendenhall, George, Blue Cross of Georgia/Columbus Inc.
Metzger, Paul, Federal Reserve Bank of Atlanta
Miller, James H., Jr., Georgia Power Company
Miller, Richard, *Bankers Magazine*
Miller, Victoria W., The First Atlanta Corporation
Montgomery, L. C., Jr., Montgomery Ventures Ltd.
Montgomery, L. C., III, Montgomery Ventures Ltd.
Moore, Calvin, Ethyl Corporation
Morine, Bruce P., Peachtree Doors Inc.
Moye, C. Mickle, Bank of the South, Cobb County
Nelson, Robert E., Jr., Cable America Inc.
Neth, Jerry P., Cahners Publishing Company
Neutzie, William A., Ohio Credit Union League
Norwood, Samuel W., Fuqua Industries Inc.
Oliver, William E., International Business Consultants Inc.
Parham, Linda, Federal Reserve Bank of Atlanta
Parker, Beth, Gwinnett Industries Inc.

Parker, Joel, Federal Reserve Bank of Atlanta

Patterson, Thomas A., Campbell-Hausfield Division of The Scott & Fetzer Company

Peery, Charles L., The First National Bank of Florence

Peterson, Dean, Nabisco Brands Inc.

Phillips, Cecil, Rock-Tenn Company

Pierce, Jeff S., Jr., First Federal S&L of Warner Robins

Quillian, Rudolph T., Valuation Services of LaGrange

Rayl, Richard, First Equity Corporation of Florida

Rieck, Steve, Georgia Department of Community Affairs

Roach, Benjamin, Nabisco Brands Inc.

Robinson, J. William, John H. Harland Company

Rogers, George, Georgia Department of Industry and Trade

Rogers, Mark, Federal Reserve Bank of Atlanta

Rosenbaum, Mary, Federal Reserve Bank of Atlanta

Ross, John M., NCR Corporation

Rossin, Thomas E., Flagler National Bank of the Palm Beaches

Ruwe, G. Jerry, Superior Linen & Apparel Services Inc.

Sabbarese, Don, Federal Reserve Bank of Atlanta

Sack, Sidney, HBO & Co.

Samples, Bill, Fuqua Industries Inc.

Satterthwaite, Joe W., Towers, Perrin, Foster & Crosby Inc.

Scherer, Robert W., Georgia Power Company

Schmicker, Catrina, Manufacturers Hanover Trust Co.

Shell, Owen G., Jr., First American Bank of Nashville N.A.

Sheppard, Joe, First National Bank of Dalton

Sherrouse, Stella, The Chamber/New Orleans and the River Region

Smith, Fred, Commerce Union Bank

Smith, James F., Jr., Smith/Park National Bank

Smith, T. Michael, J. C. Bradford & Company

Staggs, David A., Dames & Moore

Stayman, Myron D., Al Nyman & Son Inc.

Steinhauser, Delores, Federal Reserve Bank of Atlanta

Story, Roddy L., Jr., Commerce Union Bank

Strasberg, Seymour, Wickes Companies Inc.

Stroud, John M., Greater Kingsport Area Chamber of Commerce

Stumvall, Erica, Federal Reserve Bank of Atlanta

Sullivan, Gene, Federal Reserve Bank of Atlanta

Swanson, Dean C., Standard Telephone Company
Swanson, Kay S., Standard Telephone Company
Takagi, Masaru, The Fuji Bank Ltd.
Tapp, Gary, Federal Reserve Bank of Atlanta
Taylor, Scriven, Delta South Oil & Gas Company
Teasley, Harry E., Jr., The Wine Spectrum
Tillquis, W., Atlantic Richfield Company
Topple, James H., Pattillo Construction Co. Inc.
Tucker, Edward G., Jr., Burhalter & Company, Certified Public Accountants
Uceda, Gus, Federal Reserve Bank of Atlanta
Ulrich, Robert A., Northern Trust Company
Van Schelt, Amy, Federal Reserve Bank of Atlanta
Vergara, Manuel F., Totalbank
Vincent, Carolyn H., Federal Reserve Bank of Atlanta
Volz, William J., El Paso Community College
Wadman, Wesley W., IDS Advisory
Wall, Larry, Federal Reserve Bank of Atlanta
Walsh-Kloss, Cynthia, Federal Reserve Bank of Atlanta
Walter, John D., Jr., Dow Corning Corporation
Washburn, John R., North Alabama Industrial Development Association Inc.
Waters, C. Britt, Georgia Power Company
Wells, Howard W., Jr., The Bibb Company
Westmoreland, M. J., Georgia State Bank
Whigham, Pam, Federal Reserve Bank of Atlanta
White, David L., The Hartford Insurance Group
Whitehead, David, Federal Reserve Bank of Atlanta
Wielicki, Anthony F., Eaton Corporation
Wilbanks, S. Sealy, Jr., Citibanc Group Inc.
Williams, Thomas L., McKenney's Inc.
Wilson, Gene, Federal Reserve Bank of Atlanta
Wilson, J. Miles H., Simons-Eastern Co.
Winer, Leon, Pace University Graduate School of Business
Wingate, J. Alton, Cornelia Bank
Winston, James H., LPMC
Wiser, Paul E., Sr., MACO Federal Credit Union

Wofford, William R., CTE Data Services
Woodard, George D., First American Corporation
Yaeger, Kathy, Bank of America
Zimmerman, Charles S., Citizens and Southern National Bank

Selected Bibliography

"America's Top Growth Companies." *Financial World*, August 15, 1981, pp. 32–55.

Athos, Anthony G., and Richard T. Pascale. *The Art of Japanese Management*. The S&S Co., Central Point, OR, 1981.

Bell, Daniel. *The Coming of Post-Industrial Society: A Venture in Social Forecasting*. Basic Books, New York, 1973.

————, and Irving Kristol. *The Crisis in Economic Theory*. Basic Books, New York, 1981.

Brandt, Steven C. *Entrepreneuring: The Ten Commandments of Building a Growth Company*. Addison-Wesley Publishing Co., Reading, MA, 1982.

Brown, Lester. *Building a Sustainable Society*. W. W. Norton & Co., New York, 1982.

Cass, Roger. *The World Economy (1982)—The End of the Golden Age?* NAE Research Associates, Santa Barbara, CA, 1982.

Dederick, Robert G. "Major Changes in Prospect in List of Growth Industries." *Business America*, February 22, 1982, pp. 10–11.

Drucker, Peter F. *The Concept of the Corporation*. John Day, Jr., Books, New York, 1972.

————. Toward the Next Economics & Other Essays. Harper & Row Publishers, New York, 1981.

"Front-Runners in a Restructured Economy." *Business Week*, June 1, 1981, pp. 94–98.

Gilder, George. *Wealth and Poverty*. Basic Books, New York, 1981.

Hawkins, Paul. *The Next Economy*. Holt, Rinehart, & Winston, New York, 1983.

————, James Ogilvy, and Peter Schwartz. *Seven Tomorrows: Towards a Voluntary History*. Bantam Books, New York, 1982.

Henderson, Bruce D. *Henderson on Corporate Strategy*. Abt Books, Cambridge, MA, 1979.

"How to Build a Growth Company." *Nation's Business*, October 1982, pp. 93–94.

Judson, Horace F. *Search for Solutions*. Holt, Rinehart, & Winston, New York, 1980.

Kuhn, Thomas. *The Structure of Scientific Revolution.* University of Chicago Press, Chicago, 1970.

LeBoeuf, Michael. *The Productivity Challenge: How to Make It Work for America and You.* McGraw-Hill Book Company, New York, 1982.

Levitt, Arthur, Jr. *How to Make Your Money Make Money.* Dow Jones-Irwin, Homewood, IL, 1981.

Lohr, Steve. *Overhauling America's Business Management.* McGraw-Hill Book Company, New York, 1982.

Lundstedt, Sven B., and Colglazier E. William. *Managing Innovation: The Social Dimensions of Creativity, Invention, & Technology.* Pergamon Press, Elmsford, NY, 1982.

McFarlan, Warren, and James McKenny. *Corporate Information Systems Management: The Issues Facing Senior Executives.* Dow Jones-Irwin, Homewood, IL, 1982.

Masuda, Yoneji. *The Information Society as Post-Industrial Society.* World Future Society, Bethesda, MD, 1981.

Morishima, Michio. *Why Has Japan "Succeeded"?: Western Technology and the Japanese Ethos.* Cambridge University Press, Chicago, 1965.

Morris, David. *Self Reliant Cities: Energy and the Transformation of Urban America.* Sierra Club Books, San Francisco, 1982.

Naisbitt, John. *Megatrends: Ten New Directions Transforming Our Lives.* Warner Books, New York, 1982.

Ogilvy, James A. *Many Dimensional Man: Decentralizing Self, Society, and the Sacred.* Oxford University Press, New York, 1977.

Olson, Mancur, and Hans H. Landsberg. *The No Growth Society.* W. W. Norton & Co., New York, 1974.

———. *The Rise and Decline of Nations: Economic Growth, Stagflation, & Social Rigidities.* Yale University Press, New Haven, CT, 1982.

Ouchi, William G. *Theory Z: How American Business Can Meet the Japanese Challenge.* Addison-Wesley Publishing Co., Reading, MA, 1981.

Rahn, Richard. *Special Report, The U.S. Industrial Outlook: U.S. Chamber Forecast Center.* Chamber of Commerce of the United States, Washington, DC, 1981.

Reich, Robert B., and Ira C. Magaziner. *Minding America's Business: The Decline and Rise of the American Economy.* Harcourt Brace Jovanovich, New York, 1981.

Soloman, Ezra. *Beyond the Turning Point: The U.S. Economy in the 1980s.* W. H. Freeman and Co., San Francisco, 1981–1982.

Stein, Herbert. *What Makes America Run?* Standard Oil Company, Cleveland, 1981.

Steiner, Gary H. *The Creative Organization.* University of Chicago Press, Chicago, 1965.

Thurow, Lester C. *The Zero-Sum Society: Distribution and the Possibilities for Economic Change.* Basic Books, New York, 1980.

Toffler, Alvin. *Future Shock.* Bantam Books, New York, 1971.

———. *The Third Wave.* William Morrow & Co., New York, 1980.

"The Up and Comers: The Class of 1982." *Forbes,* November 8, 1982, pp. 126–152.

Waterman, Robert H., Jr., and Thomas J. Peters. *In Search of Excellence: Lessons from America's Best Run Companies.* Harper & Row Publishers, 1982.

Wilson, Ian H. *Corporate Environments of the Future: Planning for Major Change.* Presidents Association of the American Management Associations, New York, 1976.

Index